city SAFARIS

A SIERRA CLUB EXPLORER'S GUIDE TO URBAN ADVENTURES FOR GROWNUPS AND KIDS

Carolyn Shaffer and Erica Fielder
Drawings by Erica Fielder

Sierra Club Books
San Francisco

The Sierra Club, founded in 1892 by John Muir, has devoted itself to the study and protection of the earth's scenic and ecological resources—mountains, wetlands, woodlands, wild shores and rivers, deserts and plains. The publishing program of the Sierra Club offers books to the public as a nonprofit educational service in the hope that they may enlarge the public's understanding of the Club's basic concerns. The point of view expressed in each book, however, does not necessarily represent that of the Club. The Sierra Club has some sixty chapters coast to coast, in Canada, Hawaii, and Alaska. For information about how you may participate in its programs to preserve wilderness and the quality of life, please address inquiries to Sierra Club, 730 Polk Street, San Francisco, CA 94109.

PHOTO CREDITS: All photographs are by Karen Stafford Rantzman except for the following: pages 9, 89, 100, and 127, Linda Hutchinson; and page 159, courtesy of Shoots 'n Roots.

Library of Congress Cataloging-in-Publication Data

Shaffer, Carolyn, 1943–
  City safaris.

  Bibliography: p.
    1. City children—United States.   2. Cities
and towns—United States—Interpretive programs.
3. Urban ecology (Biology)—United States—
Problems, exercises, etc.   4. Human ecology—
United States—Problems, exercises, etc.   I. Fielder,
Erica.   II. Sierra Club.   III. Title.
HT206.S53   1987   307.7'6'0973   86-28012
ISBN 0-87156-713-X
ISBN 0-87156-720-2 (pbk.)

Cover/Jacket design by Catherine Flanders
Book design by Catherine Flanders
Printed in the United States of America
10 9 8 7 6 5 4 3 2 1

Erica dedicates this book to:
Mom, who helped me raise polliwogs
and wild birds;
the memory of Dad, who encouraged
my interest in geology;
and my brother, Greg, who, after 30 years,
still remembers the names of the butterflies in
our collection.

Carolyn dedicates this book to:
Mom and Dad, who, by raising me
alternately in a big city and on a small farm,
helped me delight in
streetcars and skyscrapers
as well as fruit trees and pheasants.

ACKNOWLEDGMENTS

Among the scores of people who helped make this book possible, we especially wish to thank those who inspired us to see and experience city streets and wild places in fresh ways.

Treasure hunts, bumpersticker surveys and many other playful activities in this book sprouted from seeds planted by master educator and inventor of games Ron Jones. A number are modifications or expansions of the activities and suggestions scattered throughout his series of *Deschool Primers* (now out of print). We found Deschool Primer No. 3: *Your City Has Been Kidnapped* especially inspiring.

From the women of the Audubon Nature Training Society (ANTS), we both learned the Discovery Method of environmental education. Erica attributes her decision to work in the field of outdoor education to the inspiration of Dr. Esther Railton. The courses this pioneering environmental education professor taught at California State College at Hayward awakened Erica to the twin ideas of bringing nature into the classroom and taking students outdoors to learn. When Carolyn and a group of teenagers took a day-long walk through San Francisco with Michael Doyle, president of Interaction Associates and an expert on planning and communication, they learned that a city can be one of the best classrooms of all, yielding fascinating secrets to those who choose to look and listen.

City Safaris, an expanded and completely revised edition of our self-published *Ecology for City Kids,* is the grandchild of an environmental education program we conducted through the San Francisco Ecology Center. We thank all who were involved with us at the Center—Gil Bailie, Katsy Mason, Charlie Starbuck, Marc Kasky, and many others—for offering friendship, support and a base of operations for our work with city kids.

Both the Ecology for City Kids program and our initial book were funded by the San Francisco Foundation. We are grateful to the Foundation and its former director, Martin Paley, for catching the spirit of our work and providing the grants that launched us as an urban ecology team and made the parent book to this one possible.

The San Francisco School District's Environmental Science Center enabled us to bring our Ecology for City Kids program into public school classrooms throughout the city. We appreciate the Center not only for its sponsorship but also for providing us with such practical ideas as the make-it-yourself daypack (see Appendix).

We also thank our agents, Michael Larsen and Elizabeth Pomada, and our editor at Sierra Club Books, Danny Moses, for believing in our book and remaining enthusiastic and supportive throughout the writing and publishing process. We appreciate photographer Karen Rantzman for capturing our explorations on film; the kids at Hedge School in Berkeley and Carolyn's neighbors Lorelle, Ursi and Benji Boynton and Sally and Sarah Nelson for taking part in city expeditions and photo sessions; and our colleagues and friends, Beth Barker, Margo Nanny, Rhea Irvine and Lindy Johnson, for reviewing the manuscript at a critical stage and giving us useful suggestions for revision.

Others who gave us support and encouragement at various stages of the project include Mary Lou van Deventer, Daniel Knapp, Susan Goltsman, Dan Iacafano, Dr. William Hammerman, Meri Jaye, Eleanor McCallie Cooper, Dorothy-Gayle Grubb, Kirsten Roth, Eileen Atkinson, Mary Lawton, Vanessa Malcarne, Tom Cole, Al Magary, Paul Quinn, and Joshua Gitomer. We wish we had space to name the dozens of people and organizations who provided information and materials for use in the book. A number of them are listed at the back under Resources.

Erica expresses heartfelt gratitude to Peg McBride, and Karin and Ed Lubin who planted and harvested summer, winter and spring gardens without her so she might work on this book. She sends special appreciation to Ed whose contagious playfulness helped her add humor to the illustrations.

Carolyn thanks Sypko Andreae for putting up so gracefully with all manner of strange hours and moods during the rewrite process and for giving total support to every phase of the project. Both Carolyn and Erica appreciate the countless hours Sypko has donated over the years to keep our word processing systems running smoothly.

CONTENTS

INTRODUCTION

The city is a fact of nature, like a cave, a run of mackerel or an ant heap. —Lewis Mumford

Back in 1972, when we began putting together a program of urban ecology walks for kids, we didn't find any books that integrated the human with the natural aspects of the city. So we developed our own games and activities and later published them in the slim volume *Ecology for City Kids.* That was in 1976. Today we still haven't found another book that integrates bank buildings and bus systems with bees and butterflies, so we have rewritten and expanded our original material into *City Safaris,* gearing the text to any adult who lives or works with kids whether as parent, aunt, uncle, scout leader, camp counselor, librarian, or teacher. The book can be used to explore any size city or town.

When most people think of nature in the city, they picture parks and zoos and dandelions pushing up through cracks in the concrete. We picture these, too, but we also think of asphalt streets, granite office buildings, and mazes of underground pipes and cables. The city, for us, is as much a natural phenomenon as an artificial one. The materials of which the streets and buildings are constructed began as prehistoric jungles and ancient mountains; the systems that make a city go—its transportation, utility, communication, food, and disposal networks—parallel those found among plants and birds and insects.

We like to think of a city as a living being, a complex organism that, just like a tree, a bird, or a flowering plant, takes in energy and materials from the environment, transforms and uses these, and returns energy and matter, in different forms, to the larger environment. In working with kids, we often compare the city to a human body. Some might question whether a city, especially a big one, has a heart, but no one denies that a city has a circulatory system —several, in fact. Everything from water to watermelons and from flammable fuels to bright ideas flows in, around, and out of a city in sizable quantities.

In this book we help you and your kids see the city whole, complete with plants, animals, people, and city systems. We also help you see its connections to the rest of the planet. Most kids, and probably many grownups, don't know where their tap water comes from or how it's treated. Few could name the regions that produced the meat, fish, vegetables, fruit, and dairy products they eat daily. And many have no idea what happens to the scraps from these meals once they are tossed into the garbage can.

Kids probably know more than grownups about the grassy parks and weedy vacant lots of their city. They can, most likely, point out all the birds' nests on a block and guide their friends to the best salamander shelters. But few know how the plants and bugs and birds depend on one another in the fragile web of life. Not many could describe an urban ecosystem, their own or that of their animal and plant friends.

In his classic *The Culture of Cities,* Lewis Mumford describes the city not only as a fact of nature but also as a conscious work of art that contains within it "many simpler and more personal forms of art." On your urban safaris, you might find yourselves noticing for the first time the beauty in such ordinary objects as a manhole cover or a cluster of potted geraniums on a front porch.

In *City Safaris* we show how you and your kids can explore your neighborhood and city through simple walks, games, and projects. You'll learn how to peek under rocks to find hidden animal homes and slip undetected into downtown streets to observe the strange behavior of Homo sapiens. You'll find out how to go on treasure hunts, play three-story street games, and raise a worm farm in a box. You'll discover how to find art at your feet, turn trash into treasure, and travel around the world with your brown-bag lunch. And through all these trips and games, you and your kids will discover the wonderfully woven webs of human, plant, and animal life that keep your city alive and as healthy as a city can be.

HOW TO USE THIS BOOK
City Safaris is more an explorer's kit than a step-by-step guide to the city environment. It's a toolbox of games, hints, and how-tos. With its contents you can design any number of city explorations to suit your needs and interests. You can create half-hour walks around the block for four-year-olds, taking with you nothing but crayons and paper, or you can design month-long environmental study projects for fourteen-year-olds in which they use cameras and tape recorders, conduct interviews and opinion polls, and perform library research.

The activities tend to follow a certain order, with the simpler games and projects and those that can be performed close to home preceding the more complex ones and those that take you and your kids farther afield. You need not follow this order. Each game, worksheet, and project can stand alone and be performed in any order.

If you are exploring with just one or two kids, you might choose an activity at random and carry it out with

---
✳

When we try to pick out anything by itself, we find it hitched to everything in the Universe. One fancies a heart like our own must be beating in every crystal and cell.
—John Muir, *My First Summer in the Sierra*

little planning or structure. This improvisational approach doesn't work so well if you happen to be a teacher or group leader working with twenty-five fifth-graders or a troop of Boy or Girl Scouts. For those of you who work with groups, we provide sample worksheets and suggest ways you can operate in teams with clear tasks. We also include suggestions for follow-up activities and projects you can conduct when you return to your meeting place or classroom. The worksheets in *City Safaris* are intended as examples only. We encourage you to reword and rearrange the questions and instructions so they work best for your particular group and neighborhood. If you're exploring with very young children or those who do not yet read, you can use the sample worksheets as leaders' guides, raising the questions and explaining the tasks orally.

Throughout the book we have sprinkled ticklers: curious facts, wise sayings, scratch-the-head-type questions, inspiring examples of what youth groups have done to enliven and improve their cities, and suggestions for projects that you and your kids might take on.

We hope the questions we pose will lead you and your kids to raise other questions. Perhaps they will prompt your sons, daughters, scouts, or students to scurry off to the encyclopedia, the library, or an interview with a neighbor or a local expert to find the answers. It's a sneaky way to teach kids about research.

The curious facts and statistics provide useful background information on city people, plants, animals, and systems. They also may help you impress your kids with your vast store of knowledge.

Because all kids—and grownups—do not learn in the same way, we encourage you to approach the activities included here in a variety of ways. Some kids are whizzes with words and logical thinking; others express themselves best in images or through movement and the building of models. You might offer kids a choice in the way they record their observations. Let *them* decide whether they sketch what they see, build a model of it, act it out, or write about it. Later, you might ask them to record the same

observations in a different manner. Those who express themselves best in nonverbal ways might find they can put their observations into words better after they have made sketches, built models, or created dramas.

Kids labeled slow learners might surprise both you and themselves with their bright ideas and sensitive insights. Because our culture and our schools are geared to verbal, analytical thinking, the artists and intuitives are often mislabeled slow when they simply learn and express themselves in ways that aren't acknowledged and rewarded.

1. *sharpening* CITY SENSES

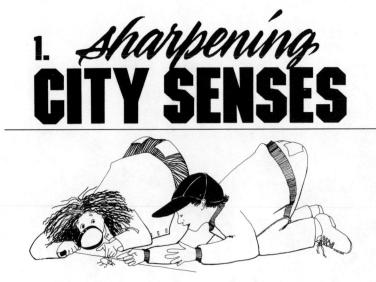

MOST OF THE TIME WE WALK AROUND blind to our surroundings, screening out as much as ninety percent of the sights, sounds, smells, and textures that bombard us. We must do this to some extent to survive, expecially in a noisy, crowded city. But such protective blindness can so deaden us to our environment that we lose touch with the beautiful and the playful as well as the ugly and the unpleasant. By sharpening our physical senses and using them selectively, we can reawaken to the wonder, beauty, and humor that exist side-by-side with the harsh realities of the urban environment.

The games, walks, and other activities in this chapter help us and our children not only notice but play with the sights, sounds, smells, tastes, and textures of our city, be it large or small. For the most part, these activities can be conducted indoors as well as out, with small or large groups, and with kids of any age.

SEE, HEAR, SMELL, TOUCH

Two of the most enthusiastic groups we led on our Outdoor City Senses Walk were teachers taking a university extension course and junior high students from an inner-city school. Age does not matter with these activities. Grownups and teenagers often welcome the chance to be children again, relating to their environment with all their senses.

As pleasurable as tasting can be, we usually do not include it in our City Senses walks simply because we don't want to encourage kids to put unknown things in their mouths. The city is full of edible plants, however, including many common weeds, and a tastes walk could be fun, full of surprises, and perfectly safe if guided by someone knowledgeable about the local flora.

Indoors Test Run

To test the sharpness of your kids' senses before heading out, try a series of brief indoor seeing, hearing, smelling, and touching tests. All the equipment you need is *paper* and either *pencils or crayons.* Once your kids are settled in comfortable places, ask them to close their eyes, relax, and take a couple of deep breaths. Then take them through each sense, except taste, starting with hearing and ending with sight. Here are suggestions for how you might guide your kids on their journey:

———————————— * ————————————

We know that cameras record sights and tape recorders record sounds. What records smells? Can smells be recorded at all? How do smoke alarms work? Do they detect the smell of smoke?

●*Hearing.* Close your eyes. Pay attention to the sounds you hear. How many different sounds can you count? Can you tell what each one is? How would you describe each sound?

●*Touching.* With your eyes still closed, feel your fingertips. Move them across the surfaces of various objects around or on you—your shirtsleeve, your chair, your crayons. Can you feel the differences in texture? How would you describe each one?

●*Smelling.* With your eyes still closed, sniff first a piece of paper, then a pencil or crayon. If you have a book nearby, sniff that also. Can you notice the differences in smell? What words would you use to describe these?

●*Seeing.* Now, open your eyes and look around the room. What object catches your eye? Notice its shape, color, and size. Does it have a pattern in it? How would you describe the shape and pattern? Can you find this shape and pattern repeated anywhere else in the room? Look for an object of a different size, shape, and color and do the same. What is the shape, color, and size of the room itself?

As a follow-up to this, have the kids draw, describe, or make rubbings of the sights, sounds, smells, and textures they discovered. (See page 9 for instructions for making rubbings.) This is a good way to sneak in a vocabulary exercise. Have you ever tried to describe a smell using words other than *sweet* or *sour?*

HOW TO MAKE A RUBBING

You may not have to teach this to kids. They've probably already made rubbings of nickels or dimes or of whatever stray objects they find on their desks.

The only materials you need to make a rubbing are a *pencil or a crayon* and *a piece of paper.* Instructions are simple. If the object is a fresh leaf or something else soft or limp, position it

on a firm surface. (See How to Make a Clipboard on page 173.) Place the paper over the surface you want to rub. Using the side of a crayon or pencil tip, rub slowly back and forth across the paper-covered object until the pattern of the surface becomes visible.

Leaves with clearly defined veins make good subjects for practicing pencil rubbings. Suggest that your kids make both crayon and pencil rubbings of the same object and compare them. Experiment with other media such as charcoal or pastels.

You and your kids can develop any number of projects using rubbings. You might make a wall chart of the different kinds of trees in your neighborhood, using leaf rubbings to identify each. Or you might concoct guessing games with mystery rubbings from the neighborhood. Rubbings of historical plaques and tombstones can lead to studies of your city's history.

Outdoor City Senses Walk

When you and your kids head outdoors to sharpen your senses, you still need only the simplest equipment: *paper* and either *crayons or pencils*. You may want to make a simple map of the area you are about to explore and bring that along as well. If you plan to mark your finds on the map, you'll need a clipboard or other firm backing for it. (Turn to page 173 for instructions for making your own clipboard.) You can turn this into a more sophisticated expedition if you wish by bringing along a magnifying lens, a cassette recorder, and a camera.

The beauty of this City Senses walk is that, even with groups of fifteen or more, it can become a spontaneous event and requires only a small area for exploration: a backyard, a stretch of sidewalk, or one corner of a schoolyard. Small groups can share a single map or not bother with one at all.

If you're a group of six or more, you might prefer to divide into teams and ask each team to choose both a recorder and a reporter. Each recorder can make a map of the area to be explored, or you can draw a map beforehand and give a copy to each team recorder. The recorder marks the team's finds on the map. At the end of the expedition, when the teams regroup, the reporters describe their team's finds to the other teams.

Depending on how much time you have, your teams can investigate all the senses in two or three hours, or you can explore a different one each day. You can

---------------------------   ✳   ---------------------------

Ants have built-in compasses that depend on highly developed senses. They smell extremely faint odors and can recognize chemicals through the touch of their sensitive antennae. If you disrupt their trail by rubbing your finger across it, the ants will use these senses to locate their trail beyond your finger scent.

—Margaret O. Hyde, *Animal Clocks and Compasses*

also add more teams by dividing the seeing category into subcategories and assigning a team to each. Subcategories might include landmarks, colors, shapes, and patterns. At the end of each outing, if time permits, the teams can take turns leading the whole group to their most interesting finds.

Another variation of this city senses game involves playing all but the seeing parts of it blindfolded. Team members could either choose one person as a seeing-eye guide or pair off and take turns guiding one another.

Returning and Sharing

When you return, make one big map of the area explored. While each team's reporter describes the team's finds, the team recorder can mark them on the big map. Team members might talk about how they felt about their finds. Did they like them all? Did they find some of them unpleasant? Were they surprised to find certain objects, sounds, smells, and textures? Which would they like to have more of in their environment? Which less?

Some of the discoveries you and your kids make on your City Senses walks could lead you into new avenues of investigation. Your rubbings of manhole and water main covers imbedded in the street or sidewalk might prompt you to investigate the underground city: the network of sewer systems and pipelines on which our lives depend.

We find our City Senses walks lend themselves well to art projects, especially collages, and guessing games. We encourage the different teams to combine their drawings, rubbings, photos, and found objects in one large collage or display. Sometimes we ask the sights team to make a giant landmarks map illustrated with their drawings or photos. If the sounds team has collected street sounds on tape, we might use these with the whole group in a crayon drawing exercise. While we play the tape, we ask the kids to express their responses to the sounds in spontaneous crayon drawings.

Don't leave the smells or textures teams out. Ask them to organize guessing games. A textures test is easy to arrange. The team members need simply put several found objects with different textures and shapes into a paper bag and ask the other kids to reach, one at a time, into the bag, feel the objects, and guess their identities. A sniff test is also fairly simple to conduct. We give instructions on page 16.

While we've never tried it, we have imagined producing, with kids, a city senses performance for family, friends, and neighbors. Here's our fantasy of how each team would contribute to a:

CITY SENSES ART EXHIBIT AND SYMPHONY PERFORMANCE

- *Sights team.* Mount and display sketches and photos of neighborhood landmarks, shapes, and patterns.

- *Textures team.* Mount and display crayon and pencil rubbings of neighborhood surfaces.

- *Smells team.* Create a collage display of the leaves, flowers, and soil collected from the neighborhood— accessible for sniffing. Provide fresh flower arrangements for the event using scented flowers from members' home gardens.

- *Sounds team.* Provide musical accompaniment. Either improvise a city sounds symphony by mimicking the car honks, bird songs, and other street sounds detected in the neighborhood or record these sounds and produce a taped musical score.

- *Sights and sounds team together.* Produce a multimedia slide-tape show of sights and sounds from the neighborhood.

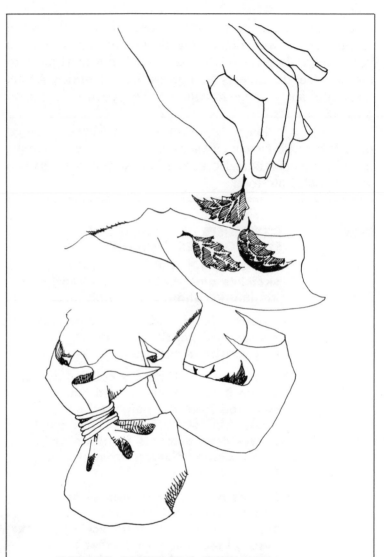

HOW TO CONDUCT A SNIFF TEST

You can organize a sniff test with *scented leaves and flowers* you have gathered outdoors or with *aromatic ingredients from the kitchen.* If collecting outdoors, remind your kids to pick only one or two leaves or flowers from each tree or bush to avoid disturbing the natural balance and beauty of the environment. If using kitchen ingredients, check your spice shelf for bay leaves, basil, nutmeg, and other herbs and spices with noticeable scents. Tea bags can serve as ready-made testers.

In three easy steps, you can make small bags or sachets from *scraps of thin cloth* and either *rubber bands or short lengths of string or twine:*

1. Cut a 6-in square of light cotton cloth for each ingredient you wish to include.

2. Place a small handful of an herb, spice, or other aromatic substance in the center of each square.

3. Make bundles out of each and secure with a piece of string or twine or a rubber band.

To conduct the test, label each sachet with a number. On an index card or any separate piece of paper, list the numbers and the ingredients corresponding to them. Keep this key out of sight until all members of the group have tried to guess the substance inside each sachet. When the group members have finished guessing, let them check their answers against the key.

Tip: Squeezing the sachets helps make the scents stronger.

You can turn this test into a practical project by making sachets for dresser drawers and closets. Ask your kids to investigate which scents tend to keep moths out of clothing and linens.

2. coping with change
CREATING CHANGE

TRAFFIC LIGHTS CHANGE, AND DOZENS of cars hurtle past. Jobs change, and the families we grew up with move. Vacant lots change, or disappear, and modern condominiums arise.

Any one of these shifts could spell disaster or opportunity for the people and other living things involved, depending on how well they have learned to detect, cope with, and create change.

Before we—and the children we live and work with—can respond to change effectively we must notice it. That's why it's important to sharpen our city senses. After one or two City Senses walks, we begin to pay attention to our surroundings, to notice the caterpillars turning into butterflies, the neighborhood shops changing hands, and the traffic patterns shifting. But noticing change isn't enough. Understanding and responding to it is what counts.

Change comes in two basic varieties: the kind we can control and the kind we can't. If our kids grow up thinking there's just one kind, the change that happens to them rather than the kind they make happen, they may begin to feel like powerless specks of life in a universe beyond control. Such feelings of powerlessness can lead to apathy, despair, and a desire to escape or destroy.

We've learned that even in a big, anonymous city, kids need not grow up feeling powerless. Opportunities abound for us grownups and our kids to create change as well as cope with it, to put our personal stamp on the world even in a small way. We need only be aware of the possibilities and willing to make the first move. We can plant a garden, make friends with our neighbors, clean up a street, or organize a food-buying service for senior citizens.

To help kids find a balance between going along with change and creating change we must first teach them to distinguish between the two kinds of changes: those within their control and those beyond it. Then we need to help them learn through experience that even the changes outside our control do not leave us without choice. We can always choose how we will respond to an event or decision. If rain falls on our picnic, we can be grumpy about it and waste the afternoon or be clever and find something fun to do indoors. Learning to cope with change can be as creative a process as initiating change. Both require imagination.

The children at an elementary school where one of us, Erica, taught environmental studies for several years, faced a classic case of change beyond their control. The school board in the small coastal town where these children lived decided to build a middle school on the acre of open space next to their elementary school. To the board this was vacant property in a prime location for a new school. To the kindergarten-through-fifth-grade kids at the existing school this lot was home to the many plants and animals they had studied over the last two years with Erica.

Wild lilies, irises, blue-eyed grass, and some plants Erica had rarely found elsewhere lived on this un-tamed acre of land soon to become a parking lot and playing

**When are you most energetic? Least
energetic? Try charting and graphing
your energy levels throughout the day.**

──────────────────────   ✳   ──────────────────────

field for the new school. It included habitats ranging from
cattail marsh to grassland to a meadow-forest transition
area, each supporting a different community of plants and
animals.

Because Erica lived in a different town and
visited the school only twice a week, she didn't learn of the
construction plans until a few days before the bulldozers
moved in. Since she had no time to arrange to save any
portion of the lot itself, she did the next best thing. Erica
worked with the children in the ten classes she visited to
salvage as many wild plants as possible by transplanting
them to other corners of the school grounds.

On the final two days before construction
began, students, parents, and teachers lugged wheelbar-
rows, buckets, and shovels from home to the vacant lot.
Then class after class of schoolkids worked with Erica digging the grasses, small bushes, and flowering plants and
doing their best to transplant each to a habitat similar to the
one from which it came. Some students gave up their recess
and part of their lunch hour to help with the project.

Not only did the students discover that they
could take an active role in responding to inevitable change,
but they also learned lessons about ecology and habitat that
many would never forget. Each student carrying a clump of
clover or grass from one site to another knew that only if
he or she identified the habitat correctly and matched it
would the plant have a chance of surviving.

The next day, several teachers at the school

──────────────────────   ✳   ──────────────────────

**If you conducted an archaeological dig
in your neighborhood, what might you
find?**

encouraged their students to write poems about the event. Later, students read a selection of the poems on a local radio show. Three years after the great transplant adventure, kids who had participated were still proudly showing Erica where the plant survivors lived.

The games and activities in this chapter help you and your kids brainstorm about change, observe it, experience it, and initiate it—indoors and outdoors, in any weather, with any size group and any age kids.

DISCOVERING CHANGE

Before leading kids outdoors to look for change, ask them to sit quietly for a few minutes and notice the changes taking place both in the room and inside themselves.

INDOOR CHANGE CHECKLIST

- **Look around. What in this room is changing?**

- **How have you changed this room since you entered it?**

- **Over what changes in this room do you have control?**

- **If you could change anything you wanted in this room, what would you change?**

- **Look inside yourself. (Use your imagination.) What in you is changing?**

- **If you could change anything you wanted about yourself, what would you change?**

- **Over what changes in yourself do you have control?**

Now, ask the kids to brainstorm about the different kinds of change they might find if they looked for change outdoors.

To get you started, here's a list of changes to seek. Add your own ideas.

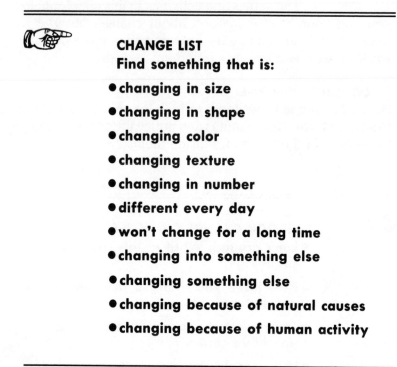

CHANGE LIST
Find something that is:

- **changing in size**

- **changing in shape**

- **changing color**

- **changing texture**

- **changing in number**

- **different every day**

- **won't change for a long time**

- **changing into something else**

- **changing something else**

- **changing because of natural causes**

- **changing because of human activity**

You can turn your list into a City Changes Treasure Hunt and use it as a tool to explore your neighborhood. On page 67 you will find tips for leading treasure hunts.

CHARTING CHANGE—INDOORS AND OUTDOORS
For a simple change-related project, you might ask your coexplorers to chart the change in temperature—either indoors or outdoors—over the course of one day. Place a weather thermometer in a spot protected from direct sun and, if possible, from blasts of heat or cold. Help the children make a temperature chart and ask one or more of them to

record the temperature on it every hour on the hour throughout the day. Later, show them how to make a graph of the temperature changes over time. For instructions and further suggestions, see How to Chart and Graph Change on page 24.

OTHER CHANGE GAMES AND PROJECTS

- Plant bean seeds in three different locations, inside and out, and see which grows the fastest.

- Stake out one square meter of a vacant lot at the first sign of spring and observe the changes that take place in a month. Count the grasses, flowers, and bugs at the start and finish of the project. Take pictures if you have a camera.

- Plant a flower box with different kinds of seeds and count the days to sprouting, flowering, and going to seed for each.

- Change the way you go to school, work, or play and notice new things about your neighborhood and city.

- Find out what your neighborhood looked like fifty years ago. Talk to parents, grandparents, neighbors, and local oldtimers. Make a model or diorama showing the way it used to be. (See How to Make a Diorama on page 26.)

- Paint your faces or put on costumes and notice how people's responses to you change—and how you feel differently about yourselves.

HOW TO CHART AND GRAPH CHANGE

Paper and pen—or felt-tip markers— are all you need to help your kids make graphs of the changes they choose to track. If you plan to display the graphs, use *oversize paper or poster board.* Colored markers work best if you are tracking several variables.

The example illustrated here includes a bar graph and a line graph, two of

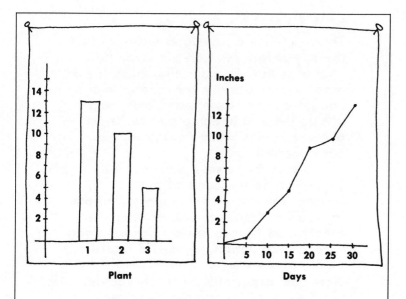

Plant

Inches

Days

the most common methods of charting change. The bar graph shows the difference in the heights of three bean plants, each grown for thirty days in locations with different amounts of light. The line graph shows how one of the plants grew in height over thirty days.

Ask your kids how they might transfer the information about the other two plants from the bar graph to the line graph. Here's where colored markers would come in handy.

If you want to provide more of a challenge, ask your kids to figure out what kinds of information the bar graph represents better than the line graph and vice versa. Investigate other kinds of graphing methods with them and the types of change these would best illustrate.

HOW TO MAKE A DIORAMA

The next time a rainstorm washes out the city safari you had planned, show your kids how to make dioramas. It's a great indoor activity for children old enough to use scissors and glue, and allows them to imagine and construct outdoor scenes while having to wait out a storm inside.

You may have seen dioramas on your visits to museums of natural history. They are scenic representations in which sculpted, cutout, or otherwise constructed figures are displayed, along with lifelike details, against a realistic painted background. Sometimes dioramas, especially those of wildlife, are life-sized. More often they are small-scale replicas of the scenes they are representing. Tiny dioramas constructed inside decorated egg-shaped containers with windows were popular Victorian-age toys.

To make a diorama you need the following materials:

- A *sturdy cardboard box* with sides at least four inches high. A shoe box is ideal.
- *Paper* for constructing figures and, if you wish, for decorating the box.
- *Scissors.*
- *Glue, tape, or clay.*
- *Plastic wrap or wax paper.*
- *Small natural objects* (fallen leaves, dry twigs, stones, and such) that can be collected without harming any living things.
- *Poster paints and small paintbrushes* (optional).
- *Photographs from magazines* and other sources (optional).

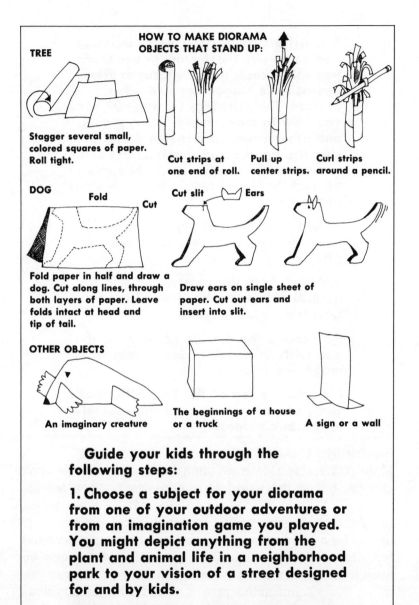

TREE

HOW TO MAKE DIORAMA OBJECTS THAT STAND UP:

Stagger several small, colored squares of paper. Roll tight.

Cut strips at one end of roll.

Pull up center strips.

Curl strips around a pencil.

DOG

Fold

Cut

Cut slit

Ears

Fold paper in half and draw a dog. Cut along lines, through both layers of paper. Leave folds intact at head and tip of tail.

Draw ears on single sheet of paper. Cut out ears and insert into slit.

OTHER OBJECTS

An imaginary creature

The beginnings of a house or a truck

A sign or a wall

Guide your kids through the following steps:

1. Choose a subject for your diorama from one of your outdoor adventures or from an imagination game you played. You might depict anything from the plant and animal life in a neighborhood park to your vision of a street designed for and by kids.

2. Cut one end off a sturdy cardboard box.

3. Use either paint or colored paper and magazine cutouts to depict a realistic scene on the inside of the box.

4. Construct figures for the foreground. You can make these from paper that you fold, score, glue, and cut or from photos from magazines and other sources. The drawings on page 27 show you how to make model trees, plants, and other stand-up paper objects. Be sure the figures you construct are small enough to fit into the box. They should be slightly less in height than the sides of the box.

5. Add small natural objects such as twigs, leaves, or stones for a realistic effect.

6. Attach both the constructed and the natural objects to the floor of the box with tape, glue, or clay.

7. Decorate the outside of the box, if you wish, with paint, colored paper, or magazine cutouts.

8. Cover the top of the box with plastic wrap or wax paper. Tape this securely to the box's sides.

IMAGINING CHANGE

In the physical world we are often stuck with things we can't change, but in the world of our imagination we are all-powerful. With our imaginations we can become bears, brooks, or bean sprouts. We can imagine what it must feel like to be a towering city highrise or a tiny neighborhood ant. Best of all, we can imagine our world to be any way we want it and hundreds of different ways.

Imagining provides kids with a marvelous way to feel large and powerful in a world in which they often feel small and helpless. But more than that, it gives kids—and us grownups, too—a way to begin creating, in nonimaginary ways, the kind of world, city, and neighborhood we want. Any creative endeavor, whether it be planning a trip, building a bird feeder, writing a poem, or organizing a recycling program, begins with imagination: a mental picture of, or a daydream about, what we want to do. Throughout this book, we sprinkle ideas about how you and your kids can use your imagination to play games, solve puzzles, and empathize with creatures different from yourselves. In Wild Places in Parks and Parking Lots we suggest you and your kids become bean sprouts (page 35) and give you pointers on how to guide such an imaginary journey (page 64).

Here are some other ideas for how you and your kids can use your imaginations to understand your city and its changes better:

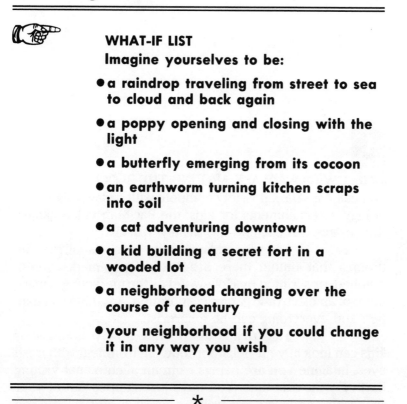

WHAT-IF LIST
Imagine yourselves to be:

● **a raindrop traveling from street to sea to cloud and back again**

● **a poppy opening and closing with the light**

● **a butterfly emerging from its cocoon**

● **an earthworm turning kitchen scraps into soil**

● **a cat adventuring downtown**

● **a kid building a secret fort in a wooded lot**

● **a neighborhood changing over the course of a century**

● **your neighborhood if you could change it in any way you wish**

＊

Plant a tree on a young child's birthday. Every time that child has another birthday measure both the tree and the child.

3. *neighborhood* ADVENTURES

I. WILD PLACES

HOW CAN A WALK AROUND THE BLOCK, even when you call it a safari, possibly compete with today's high-technology entertainments for kids: the Pac-Man video games, the Sesame Streets, and the Disney Worlds?

Consider this: A city block is alive. The dramas that unfold there are not programmed, choreographed, or scripted by Hollywood or the marketing department of an electronic games corporation. Anything can happen and everything can be a surprise.

The trick is discovering how you and your kids can look at your neighborhood environment with fresh eyes. Imagine you are beings from an alien planet visiting Earth for the first time. You have just stepped out of your spaceship, and you are walking down a city street. You wonder at the strangeness of the place and find yourself flooded with questions. What are those wires strung between buildings and tall poles? And those wheeled, metal boxes lining the sides of the street and speeding down its center? How can soft, green leafy things manage to grow out of hard concrete? And how can that little black creature with the eight legs crawl off a ledge, drop into midair, and hang there without touching the ground?

In this and the following two chapters, we take you and your kids into the wilds of your own neighborhood, exploring first the bugs and green things living there, then the street life—two-legged, four-legged, and four-wheeled—and finally the individual people.

WILD PLACES IN PARKS AND PARKING LOTS

Nature in the city means more than just parks and ponds and moss in the sidewalk cracks. It includes the very stones of which the corporate headquarters and bank buildings are built. Imagine the size hole in the mountains where these stones were quarried. Try to measure the forests from which trees were logged for all the floors, fence posts, wood frame houses, telephone poles, and tabletops throughout your city. Think of the ancient swamps dredged up from deep within the earth to make asphalt streets and playgrounds in just one of thousands of cities across the country.

Now imagine the birds, squirrels, salamanders, butterflies, ants, bees, gophers, raccoons, beetles, earthworms, grasses, shrubs, trees, and mushrooms that find livable space between stone and asphalt. Add thousands of people to these populations. Include sunlight, rain, air, and you have a highly complex set of interdependencies known as an ecosystem.

To explore the teeming ecosystems within your city, try a new method of walking down the street. Let

---

✳

Few virgin forests are left in the state of New York. One of the largest is a stand of hemlock trees in the New York Botanical Garden in the Bronx, New York City.

—Environmental Action Coalition, *City Trees, Country Trees*

your mind relax and your feet slow. Try inspecting the gutter or peering along the angle where the buildings join the sidewalk.

If you still have trouble locating wild creatures, ask a neighborhood kid. Many are authorities on such matters and can show you where ladybugs prowl, salamanders hide, or miner's lettuce grows. A fifth-grader from a school at the foot of San Francisco's Potrero Hill proudly guided us to Polliwog Creek. This flourishing natural habitat, well known to our friend and his schoolmates, was ignored by or invisible to most adults in the area. The "creek" we found turned out to be no more than a trickle of water that flowed down the hill and behind a row of industrial buildings and ended in a pond no larger than a mud puddle. Not the sort of place you'd choose for a picnic site. We had to pick our way through heaps of junked equipment and rusted cables to reach it. Once there, however, we discovered a multitude of beetles, spiders, and salamanders and, indeed, a swarm of polliwogs in the pond.

Our greatest nature-in-the-city challenge involved exploring the neighborhood surrounding San Francisco's former Washington Irving Elementary School. Bounded by the "topless" district, the financial district, the freeway, and a cluster of warehouses, it appeared hopelessly devoid of wildlife when we first surveyed it. Yet, one block from this school we discovered one of our most productive urban wild places: the untended edges of a parking lot beneath the freeway on-ramp.

Twice a day for five days in a row we led different groups of children to this unlikely nature study site. Each time, with shouts of delight, our charges discovered clusters of insect eggs, a bird's nest, and the caterpillar, pupa, and adult stages of moths and butterflies. Both kids and grownups marveled that so much life could survive the heavy auto exhaust and traffic noise of the freeway overhead and the urban congestion on all sides.

In this chapter, you'll learn how to help your kids understand the birds, bugs, flowers, food chains, and ecosystems they discover in treetops and vacant lots. You'll

Why are tree leaves different shapes?
What causes leaves to fall?

———————————— ✳ ————————————

also find instructions for using one of the most powerful of our human learning tools: the imagination.

Although we present the activities in an order that moves roughly from observation to empathy to analysis to synthesis, you may carry out the activities in any order. Each game and worksheet can stand by itself.

In Teams and Trackers, a three-story street game, you and your kids prowl your neighborhood noticing the wildlife at three levels and figuring out a few basic connections. In Becoming a Bean Sprout and Creeping Like a Cat you use imagination and movement to become the living things you have observed, and, for a change, you look at the world from their perspectives. Now that you have developed empathy with these creatures, the chapter guides you and your kids to a closeup look at the strange and marvelous worlds of plants and insects. It offers pointers on collecting bugs and flowers and examining them scientifically. Finally, to help you put the bugs, plants, and people together, it provides a series of ecology games that reveal, amid much leaping and laughing, the relationships between the creatures you've been observing and their connections to you.

The two How-tos at the end of this section provide practical suggestions for guiding kids through two bean sprout adventures—one biological, the other imaginary.

TEAMS AND TRACKERS: EXPLORING NEIGHBORHOOD NICHES

Naturalists studying forest ecology often refer to three life zones: ground level, understory, and canopy. You can adapt this three-tiered approach to the study of your neighborhood ecology. In this chapter you'll find a three-story street game that helps you and your kids track down the wildlife in your neighborhood. In the following chapter a similar

WHAT'S UNDERFOOT?

1. Look at the ground around your feet. What plants do you see? List or draw three or more of them.

2. Look for animals underneath leaves and sticks. Turn over stones and spread the grass. List or draw three or more of the animals you find.

3. Conduct a small animal and plant survey. First, place a sheet of paper on the ground where you notice plants and animals. At each corner of the sheet place a pebble, twig, or other marker. Now remove the paper and count all the living things you find in the marked-off area. How many plants? _____ How many animals? _____

4. Find an animal home on your plot and draw a picture of it. (Hint: Look closely. Some animals are tiny.) Can you tell from its size and shape what animal lives there? Name the animal: _____

5. Find three leaves on or near your plot that are different shapes and sizes. Draw or outline the leaves. Examine them for tiny animals, nibble marks, and eggs. Include these in your drawing. Crush an edge of each leaf and smell it. Below the drawing of the leaf, write one or two words that describe its scent. Find the shrubs or trees to which each leaf belongs.

type of game provides you with a method for investigating the human and built environment.

Although we present these activities in sample worksheet form, you and your coexplorers may wish to use them in less structured ways. You might, for example, turn them into treasure hunts (see page 67). If you're a group of six or more, divide into teams and commission each team to investigate a different mini-environment. Also, try playing these games at different locations in the city and comparing your results. How many different kinds of wild places can you find?

IMAGINING AND MOVING

> *empathy ('em-pe-the) n.: the capacity for participating in another's feelings or ideas.*

As powerful as the imagination is by itself, combined with movement, this tool is doubly effective. We often use it with children to generate empathy for plants, animals, and people.

By both imagining how squirrels, spiders, or blades of grass feel and moving about like them, kids not only learn to identify with and appreciate the wild creatures they share their neighborhood with but they also grow to love and care for these creatures. Through imagining and moving games, even the scariest snakes and spiders can begin to feel more like allies than enemies. Chapter 5 provides ways to use these types of games for developing empathy with different kinds of people.

Becoming a Bean Sprout gives children the inside story on how green plants grow from small, hard seeds to tall, leafy stalks. In Cat Sneak, they practice the predatory and protective behaviors of city animals. Both activities help children learn, with their muscles as well as their imaginations, what life might be like for living creatures that don't happen to be human. Once children have felt the roots of a bean sprout and crept around on cat's

WHAT'S AT EYE LEVEL?

1. Look around you at eye level. What plants do you see? List or draw three or more of them.

2. What animals do you see at eye level? List or draw three or more of them.

3. Look at the animals closely. By what means are they moving? List the ways.

4. Find an animal home at eye level and draw it. (Hint: Look closely. Some animals are tiny.) Can you tell from its size and shape what animal lives there? Name the animal:

_____

5. Choose a tree or bush at eye level. Examine its bark, leaves, and flowers. How many animals can you find on this plant? _____

6. Find three things on your plant that might be food for the animals you see. List or draw them. Examine them for nibble marks and eggs. Look for the animal that might eat them.

7. Choose one item from your list or set of drawings in the task above and circle any of the following words that describe it:

Scent: sweet / sour / sharp / stinky
*Texture:*hard/soft/sticky/prickly/ furry / rough / smooth / slippery / squishy

8. Look around at the other trees and bushes you can see from where you are standing. Are any of these plants about the same size as the one you

chose to study? If so, how many of this size plant can you count? _____
How many animals do you think are living on each of these plants? (Check your answer to #5.) Make an estimate: _____ If you could count the animals living on all the plants of this size that you can see, how many might you find? Make an estimate: _____

WHAT'S OVERHEAD?

1. Look above your head. What plants do you see? List or draw three or more.

2. What animals do you see overhead? List or draw three or more.

3. Look at the animals closely. By what means are they moving? List the ways.

4. Choose a tree. Examine its trunk and branches. How many branches grow from the trunk? _____

5. Look closely into the branches until you have found an animal. What is the animal doing? _____ What do you think this animal eats? _____
Who do you think might eat this animal? _____

6. Find three trees with leaves of different sizes and shapes. Draw or outline the leaves of each. Examine the leaves for small animals, nibble marks, and eggs. Include these in your drawings. Crush the edge of a leaf from each tree and smell it. Below the drawing of the leaf, write one or two words that describe its scent.

paws, they might find it hard to carelessly uproot a plant or tease an animal.

Becoming a Bean Sprout

Before children imagine themselves bean sprouts, they must know some facts about these green, growing things. You can help them learn these in a fun, easy way by showing them how to sprout their own bean seeds. (See page 63 for tips.)

Once the children know what germination and sprouting look like, you can lead them on an imaginary journey as a bean sprout. Here's an example of the wording you might use. Be sure to help your kids relax and ground themselves first. (See How to Guide an Imaginary Journey on page 64.) Whether using these words or your own, be sure to speak slowly and calmly, pausing frequently to allow the participants to let their imaginations create the pictures.

> *Imagine yourself a bean sprout planted in the cool, moist earth. Feel yourself soaking up moisture from the earth and beginning to swell. New life stirs within you. You put out a small, white shoot. This shoot becomes a stem, pushing you up, up, through the dark earth and toward the light.* (Pause.)
> *At last, you push through the last bit of soil. Breathe in the fresh air. Feel the warm sun.* (Pause.)
> *Within you two tiny leaves are growing. They grow and grow until they split the fleshy bean into two halves.* (Pause.)
> *Feel your two new leaves emerge and grow and begin to turn green in the sunlight. Imagine them using the sun's energy to make your food.* (Pause.)
> *Your stem is now strong and straight. Under the earth it is putting down roots that anchor you in the soil and soak up water and minerals. Become your roots, deep in the cool earth. Feel yourself drawing up minerals through these roots into your leaves.* (Pause.)

Sense the food from your leaves moving toward your growing tip. Feel your leaves unfurl in the sunshine. Feel your whole self soaking up the sun and swaying in the gentle breeze. (Pause.)

Become aware of what color you are and how your leaves are shaped. Look around you. Notice your surroundings. (Pause.)

Feel your roots again. Feel them spreading deep into the earth and holding you steady and straight. (Pause.)

Now slowly begin to return to your own body. Say goodbye to the bean plant's roots, its stem, and its two new leaves. Say goodbye to its home below ground and above ground. Remember, you can always return to this warm, nourishing place. (Pause.)

When you are ready, slowly open your eyes and, in silence, return to your body and the room (or earth beneath you).

Before you ask the children to talk about how it felt to be a bean sprout, you might ask them to move like one, to express with their body the stages of growth they just experienced in their imagination. Encourage them to curl up in little balls and to unfold slowly until they are standing tall and stretching and waving their arms like new green leaves. This moving and stretching, besides helping the children empathize with the sprouts, will get the kinks out of their bodies after this period of sitting or lying still.

Some children need quiet time after a guided fantasy; others can hardly wait to blurt out their feelings and discoveries. Be sensitive to the varied needs of your group.

——————————————— ✳ ———————————————

Albert Einstein's daydreaming landed him in trouble in school but later helped him develop his famous theories. His fantasy of himself riding a ray of light proved important to his discovery of the theory of relativity.

After a quiet reentry period, encourage discussion but do not force it. Here's a list of questions you might use to start discussion:

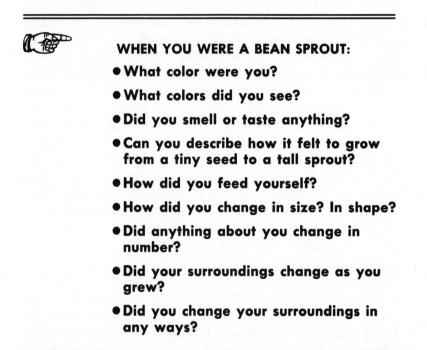

WHEN YOU WERE A BEAN SPROUT:

- **What color were you?**

- **What colors did you see?**

- **Did you smell or taste anything?**

- **Can you describe how it felt to grow from a tiny seed to a tall sprout?**

- **How did you feed yourself?**

- **How did you change in size? In shape?**

- **Did anything about you change in number?**

- **Did your surroundings change as you grew?**

- **Did you change your surroundings in any ways?**

Creeping Like a Cat

You can easily introduce imagining-and-moving games while on a neighborhood hike or at a park. When you and your kids are trudging up a slope, suggest that you all become heavy footed like a pack of mules bearing great burdens, then light footed like deer. Let the kids think of other animals they can become. You might suggest more subtle physical expressions. Try moving like the wind or the sea, fire or clouds, the sun or the moon.

Warm-ups before a movement game can help you and your kids limber up and shed inhibitions. Stretching and shaking out arms and legs may be enough. A quick game of Simon Says can also get kids' blood circulat-

ing and raise their spirit. Or, you might try the following
variation of the childhood game of Statue or Freeze. It's
designed especially to prepare kids for the game of Cat
Sneak, described below.

Start by asking the kids to begin stretching
and moving slowly about. Suddenly call out, "Freeze!" At
this command, the players must stop in midmovement.
While they hold their poses, ask them to notice the position
and balance of their bodies. Then call out, "Move!" Repeat
this two more times. During the second freeze, ask the players to notice not only what positions they are in but also
how they feel in these postures. During the third freeze, ask
the kids to imagine their bodies changing into those of cats.
Now tell them, as cats, to imagine walking along a narrow
fence rail. Ask them to feel their catness deep inside them,
to sense their paws slowly but expertly picking out the way,
to feel even the twitch of their whiskers. After a few minutes
ask all the cats to turn back into children.

Cat Sneak

In this game the players enact the dance, in nature, between
predator and prey. Because the nature you are exploring is
in the city, the predator here is a cat and its prey a mouse.
This game requires no props, only a playing area large
enough for a game of tag.

In Cat Sneak, players taking the role of cat
must sneak up, without being heard, behind their prey, a
player in the role of mouse. Besides encouraging kids to
stretch their body and imagination, Cat Sneak gives them a
chance to develop empathy with life forms other than their
own. It also teaches them about the food chain and works
well with the three ecology games described later in this
section. (See page 50.)

In the game, one kid, acting as the mouse,
stands at one end of the playing area with his or her back
to the rest of the players. These players, pretending they are
cats, stand 15 yards behind the mouse. At a signal, they
spread out and begin stalking their prey. The cats' goal is to
sneak up on the mouse and tag it before it hears them

approach. If the mouse hears an approaching player, she or he quickly turns to face the cats. The cats must instantly freeze. If the mouse sees a cat move, that player is out of the game. The game ends when either a cat tags the mouse or the mouse detects the last remaining cat moving.

Once you and your friends become practiced stalkers, you might try sneaking up on a real animal. How close do you think you can get to a wild squirrel?

FLOWERS AND BUGS UP CLOSE

The following four activities give you and your kids a chance to explore small worlds within your neighborhood, the worlds of flowers and insects. Kids, who often feel small themselves, usually welcome a chance to get down on their knees and examine creatures even smaller than they are.

Stake a Claim

How often do you and your kids sit down on a patch of grass and inspect the forests and deserts at your feet? Strange beasts stir and stalk and fly here among gnarled, scaley roots and stems within centimeters of the earth's surface. Stake a Claim helps you explore the miniature worlds that we pass by every day but usually ignore. It focuses on smallness.

In this version of the game, each participant studies a separate claim site. If you don't have enough open space available, you can adapt the game for pairs or teams. If you are using worksheets similar to the sample, make sure each kid has his or her own copy.

The materials you need for Stake a Claim are *string*—enough for a one-yard-long piece for each player—

$*$

Imagine you are an ant. How does it feel to have six legs, two antennas, and a segmented body? Imagine yourself crossing a city sidewalk. How do you find your way home? What obstacles do you encounter?

STAKE A CLAIM

1. Sit quietly by your claim. Feel the air. The air is (circle one in each pair):

   damp/dry   warm/cold   windy/still

2. Bend close to your claim and sniff the air with your eyes closed. The air smells like _____.

3. Dig your fingers into the soil. The dirt is (circle one in each pair):

   hard/soft   dry/wet   fine/coarse

4. Is the vegetation growing on your claim dense, sparse or average? (Circle one.)

5. Peer closely between the stems, roots, and rocks on your claim and find an animal. Draw this animal. What is the animal doing? _____ How does the animal protect itself? _____ Where is the animal's home? (Hint: Sometimes animals carry their homes with them.) _____

6. Look again under the rocks and around the plants of your claim. How many animals do you count there? ____

_____

7. How many plants live on your claim?

_____

Now carefully replace any plants, animals, or stones you may have moved. Leave your claim site looking just the way it did before you began exploring it.

pencils, crayons, sheets of blank paper, clipboards or other stiff backing for the paper, and, if you are using them, copies of the *worksheet.* If you have *hand lenses* or *magnifying glasses,* bring these along as well.

Before heading out to your claim site area, cut a one-meter length of string for each player. Form each piece into a loop by tying both of its ends together. When you reach your destination—a park, vacant lot, or other open space—give each player a loop of string, a clipboard, a worksheet (optional), pencils or crayons, and a sheet of blank paper. Ask each kid to choose a claim site by spreading the string loop in a wide circle over the ground. Once they have staked their claim they are ready to investigate the plants and animals living there using the worksheet or following your own set of instructions. If you have the time, encourage your kids to study a variety of claim sites—wet and dry, rocky and sandy, sunny and shady—so they can see for themselves the diversity of environments in which city plant life and wildlife thrive.

FLOWER POWER

A flower contains the reproductive parts of a plant. For a plant to reproduce, pollen from a flower of the same species must stick to the pistil of the flower being fertilized. Once this happens, a tiny cell begins to grow, extending down into the ovary of the flower. When the cell touches the ovules, or eggs, within the ovary, it fertilizes them, and they begin to develop into seeds.

Most flowers depend on insects to bring them pollen grains from other flowers of the same species. To attract insects, a flower must advertise that it provides food, usually nectar or pollen. Since insects hunt for their food by sight or smell, most flowers appear brightly colored or fragrant or both. Once an insect lands on a flower and begins actively searching for food, pollen grains stuck to its body rub off onto the pistil and the fertilization process begins.

The outermost circle of the parts of the flower is the *sepals.* Before the flower blooms, the sepals

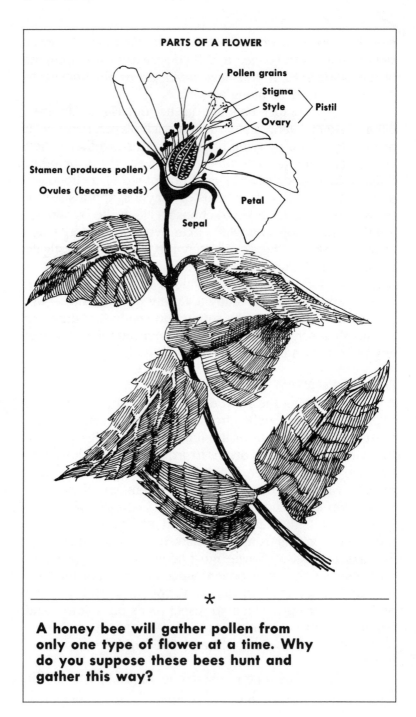

PARTS OF A FLOWER

Pollen grains
Stigma
Style
Ovary
Pistil

Stamen (produces pollen)
Ovules (become seeds)
Sepal
Petal

*

A honey bee will gather pollen from
only one type of flower at a time. Why
do you suppose these bees hunt and
gather this way?

wrap around the bud to protect it. *Petals* are usually the colorful parts of the flower that are attached just within the ring of sepals. The third ring of parts consists of *stamens*, the pollen-producing parts of a flower. They usually appear as slender filaments with nobs at the tip. In the center of the stamens stands the *pistil*, the seed-producing part of a flower. It has a sticky tip that catches pollen grains, and an *ovary* that holds the *ovules* or future seeds of the plant.

GATHERING FLOWER CLUES
Choose a brightly colored flower to study. Leave it on the plant while you observe it.

1. Count each of the flower parts. The flower has _____ petals, _____ _____ stamen, and _____ pistil(s).

2. The color of the petals is _____.

3. The color of the pollen is _____.

4. The flower is about _____ centimeters across.

5. Draw the flower and label its parts.

6. What does *reproduce* mean?

7. Look for an insect crawling in the flower's center. Can you find one? _____ _____If so, what kind is it? _____ _____Are pollen grains stuck to its body? _____

8. List three things that might attract an insect to this flower. (Hint: What attracted you?)

GOING BUGGY

Did you know that more than 88,000 insect species exist in North America alone? Despite our sharing house and garden with such multitudes, most of us know next to nothing about the creatures.

An insect has no bones. Instead, it has a hard outer skin called an *exoskeleton* to which its muscles are attached. As you can see from the illustration, an insect's body is divided into three parts: head, thorax, and abdomen. When the insect reproduces, it lays eggs. Each egg later hatches into a larva. A caterpillar, for example, is the larva of a butterfly or moth. When a larva has grown large

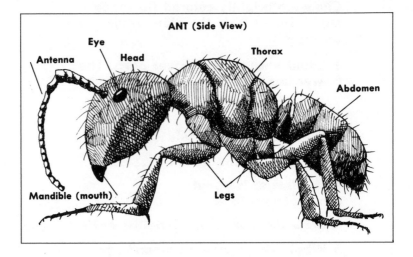

ANT (Side View)

Antenna · Eye · Head · Thorax · Abdomen · Mandible (mouth) · Legs

enough, it becomes an inactive pupa and slowly transforms into an adult: a fly, a butterfly, or a beetle, for instance.

The structure of an insect's mouth parts indicates what it eats. Below are sketches of three kinds of insect mouth parts. Many other kinds exist. How many kinds can you and your kids discover in the insects you find in your city's wild places?

Shake a Bush

Have you ever wondered how many bugs live in the bushes on your block? This activity will help you and your kids

BUG-WATCHING TIPS

- **Look for insects on warm, sunny days.**

- **Explore grassy or weedy areas where they like to live.**

- **Sit quietly and observe their activities.**

- **Use a collecting jar and a hand lens to bring insects in for a closer view.**

make an estimate. Each of you might first want to make a guess, then see whether any of you come close to the Shake a Bush estimate.

Any number of you can play this game. All you need is a *large piece of white paper or old white bedsheet; writing paper* and a *pencil;* and a *hand lens or magnifying glass.*

Before you do any counting, simply observe the wildlife you shake out of the greenery. Slide your sheet or paper under a branch of shrubbery or next to a clump of grass. Gently but firmly shake the branch or clump over the paper. When the myriad thrips, ants, spiders, beetles, and other small creatures rain down, have a look at them through the hand lens before they scurry off to the nearest hiding place—or, temporarily and carefully capture one or two in a jar for a closer view.

On your next shake, count only the spiders or only the ants that fall onto your paper or sheet. From this count estimate the numbers of ants or spiders you might find on the whole bush or in all the bushes on the site.

If you plan to visit this site throughout the season, make a chart showing changes in animal numbers

---

✳

The common housefly whines the note F in the middle octave by vibrating its wings 21,120 times a minute.

depending on time of day, available moisture, temperature, and such.

One group of kids with whom we worked invented their own variations on the game. First, they compared the number of bugs on shrubbery growing in the sun with the number on that growing in the shade. Then they compared the number on bushes with large leaves with the number on bushes with small leaves. Your kids might dream up other ways to play Shake a Bush.

PUTTING IT ALL TOGETHER: ECOLOGY GAMES

The natural world you and your kids have been exploring in the city may appear chaotic at first glance. What, your kids might wonder, do the jays squawking overhead have to do with the earwigs tucked in dark corners under rocks or the weeds growing between sidewalk cracks? Yet for centuries humans have been noticing the relationships inherent in this seemingly unkempt world of nature and, in the past century, have developed the science of ecology to study these connections.

The following three games, together with Cat Sneak (page 42), will help children grasp, through active play, the intricate relationships that weave plants, animals, and environments into living systems. To lead these games, you will need a basic understanding of the food chain concept and of the adaptative behaviors and colorings animals take on to keep the chain intact. The explanations here, while necessarily simplified, provide a starting point.

The food chain is part of a larger energy chain that starts with the sun. All living organisms need energy to move, grow, maintain themselves, and reproduce but not all organisms can use the sun's energy directly. Animals rely on plants to convert the sun's energy into usable food. They either eat plants directly or eat other animals that have eaten plants. This series of relationships, called a food chain, actually forms a cycle. The end of the chain is linked back to the plants at its beginning by bacteria and other minute life forms that swarm throughout the soil,

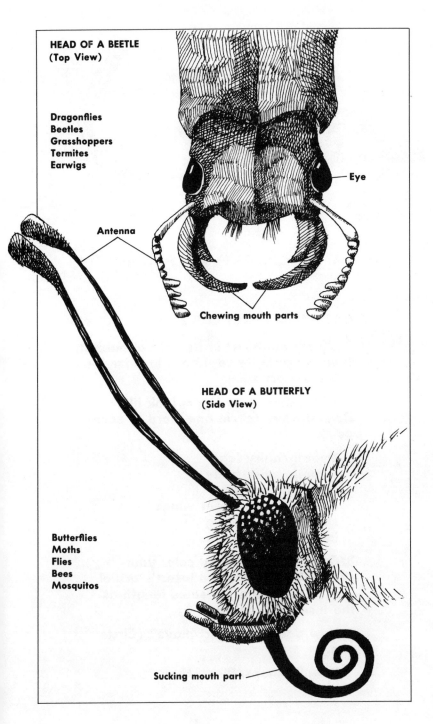

HEAD OF A BEETLE
(Top View)

Dragonflies
Beetles
Grasshoppers
Termites
Earwigs

Eye

Antenna

Chewing mouth parts

HEAD OF A BUTTERFLY
(Side View)

Butterflies
Moths
Flies
Bees
Mosquitos

Sucking mouth part

GATHERING INSECT CLUES

1. Watch an insect in its natural habitat, then temporarily capture it in a jar for closer observation.

2. What does your insect look like? Does it have (circle one word in each pair):

   smooth/hairy legs
   smooth/hairy body
   wings/no wings
   colorful/transparent wings
   shiny/dull covering
   long/short antennas

3. Draw the insect and color your sketch. To indicate the insect's actual size, draw a line the same length as the insect in your jar.

4. How does the insect move? (Circle one.)

   It walks/hops/flies/other: _____

5. How does the insect protect itself? (Circle as many as apply.)

camouflaging colors
warning colors
hard shell
pinchers
stingers
flying away
other: _____

6. What are the insect's eating habits? (Circle one in each set. Look closely!)

It has sucking/chewing mouth parts.
It is/is not eating right now.
It seems to be eating:

another insect
decomposing material
other: _____

7. Find an example of an early stage of insect growth—egg, larva, or pupa stage, for instance—and draw it.

8. How do you think the insect feels caught in a jar?

Now gently release the insect where you found it.

---
*

The ladybugs that eat the insect pests in our parks and gardens each spring have often flown hundreds of miles from their winter hibernation sites to reach our cities. Where do they get the energy to do so?

transforming fecal matter and the dead bodies of animals and plants into a rich compost in which plants thrive.

All animals, including humans, obtain their food directly or indirectly from plants. Because plants are the only organisms that can turn the sun's energy into food, they are known as primary producers. These immobile food factories constantly use solar energy to transform earth, air, and water into roots, stalks, leaves, flowers, and fruit that provide food for hungry animals. Without these green, growing things the rest of us would not be able to live, grow, and reproduce. We would be surrounded by fuel with no way to use it.

Plants use the sun's energy to provide food for the secondary producers, the animals that suck sap, chew leaves, sip nectar, or bore wood. These herbivores or plant eaters convert the original building materials and sugars from the plants into animal flesh, blood, and bone and, in turn, provide food for the third level of the food chain, the carnivores or meat eaters. These are the animals that obtain their energy and nutrients by eating animals that eat plants. Of course, nature does not always fit into neat categories. Some animals, such as we humans, eat both plants and animals and are called omnivores, which means eaters of everything.

With everything eating and being eaten by everything else, the earth begins to resemble a twenty-four-hour cafe in which no plant or animal is safe from the jaws of another. You might wonder how any organism survives the nonstop feasting. A close look at various plants and animals will provide clues to their survival. Ask your kids to

---------------------------------- * ----------------------------------

He was present for the arrival of the dinosaurs 170 million years ago; he saw the Rockies, Alps, and Appalachians push their way upward; and he was already an oldtimer when Texas oil and West Virginia coal were formed. Who is he? The lowly cockroach.

The world's insect population numbers approximately
1,000,000,000,000,000,000
—V. B. Wigglesworth, *The Life of Insects*

———————————————   ∗   ———————————————

think about why a moth's wings match the bark of its favorite tree, a yellowjacket wears the same colors as our traffic warning signs, and a delicate rosebush bears wicked thorns.

Many animals protect themselves from predators by camouflaging coloration or shape. A praying mantis's body looks like a stick, and the mottled gray fur of a fox or a coyote matches the bushes and rocks among which the animal lives. Others flash warnings to potential enemies. The yellow and black stripes of wasps warn that they may sting, and the black-and-white-striped pelts of skunks signal that these animals may emit a noxious spray. Even plants have evolved methods of warding off munching animals. They often present a potential feaster with a prickly maze of thorns and fuzz, or they secrete poisons or nasty tasting substances that deter nibbling. Stickler Camouflage and Create a Critter are two games included here that teach children about protective animal adaptations.

While prey have evolved successful protective mechanisms, predators have evolved successful hunting techniques. Cats and foxes, for instance, are stalkers; they can sneak up silently on birds and rodents and assure themselves of dinner. The game Cat Sneak, described earlier (page 42), gives kids a chance to play-act this kind of predator-prey behavior.

Other ecology games and more advanced variations of these games can be found in Lawrence Hall of Science's excellent *Outdoor Biology Instructional Strategies* (OBIS) modules. (See bibliography.)

Food Loops: A Food Chain Game
This game, best played by five to ten people, is designed to help kids better understand the intricate food relationships between plants, animals, and their environments. In it each

"It is estimated that there is scarcely a square mile of the earth's surface that does not contain some ingredient from every other mile, because of the action of wind and water."
—John H. Storer, *The Web of Life*

─────────────────────   ✳   ─────────────────────

player represents a link in the food chain. The only material you need to play the game is a *single piece of string long enough to allow a yard's length for each player.* If you wish, you may also make up sets of *name tags* and *question cards.* Before starting, review with the players the plant and animal relationships within the food chain.

Begin by measuring out the string. Tie its ends together to form a large loop. Then help the players choose their roles. Explain that they can play living things that manufacture food with sunlight (grasses, trees, flowers, mosses, etc.); animals that eat plants for their energy (birds, mice, butterflies, etc.); animals that eat other animals (cats, snakes, etc.); or animals that help decompose plants and animals (earthworms, pill bugs, flies, etc.).

You can turn this part of the preparation into a guessing game by calling out each category and asking the players to guess a member of it. Let the first to do so correctly for each category play that role in the game. As each player takes a role, ask him or her to grasp a section of the string. If you have made name tags, give the player an appropriate one. When every category is represented and each player has a role and a grip on the string, ask them to distribute themselves evenly around the string in a circle.

To play the game, you as leader pose a series of questions, asking who in the chain would be directly affected if certain events took place. Describe events that would prove harmful or fatal to certain links in the food chain. You might ask, for instance: Who would be directly affected if the air became so polluted that it blocked much of our sunlight? Who would suffer first if the earthworms, flies, and other decomposers suddenly disappeared? In re-

Which sense do you find most difficult
to describe in English? Do other
languages have more words to describe
this sense?

———————————— * ————————————

———————————— * ————————————

Map plant and animal distribution over
a five-meter-square area of a
backyard, park, or vacant lot. Do you
notice any patterns? How would you
describe these?

sponse to each question any player representing a directly affected plant or animal tugs on the string and goes through the motions of a mock death. As the others feel the tug, they also begin to fall down as if dead, the point being that the death of any one group of plants or animals will directly or indirectly affect the rest. After the players resurrect themselves, pose another question involving a different link within the chain. Continue until every player has had at least one chance to be the first to die. You can play this game repeatedly, with players shuffling roles each time.

In playing Food Loops we discovered that kids tend to become silly when they first perform their death scenes. We usually let them act out their silliness for awhile before bringing them back to a focus on the concept of the food chain and the ways in which its members relate to each other.

After you've played the game once or twice, pause to discuss the meaning of it. You might ask how humans would be affected by the breaking of certain links in the food chain, what events might cause the disappearance of certain plants and animals and what other events might cause these plants and animals to reproduce at unmanageable rates, and how humans might act to bring these populations back into balance.

This game also offers fine opportunities for drawing and storytelling. Ask kids to draw or act out the food chain dramas you've discussed. Once they understand the concepts involved, they will be able to make up their own stories—thrilling whodunits or tearjerker tragedies—

--------------------------------- * ---------------------------------

The word *ecology* was coined by a woman scientist, Ellen Swallow, in 1892. The first woman admitted to the Massachusetts Institute of Technology, Swallow recognized the need for an interdisciplinary environmental science.
—Judy Smith, *Something Old, Something New, Something Borrowed, Something Due: Women and Appropriate Technology*

Lightning helps plants eat. It touches off a series of chemical reactions that change aerial nitrogen into a form that can be used by plants. Otherwise, the 22 million tons of this aerial nutriment is insoluble and unusable.

——————————————— * ———————————————

about the breaking and healing of food chains.

Kids who like physical challenges can demonstrate the layers of a food chain by forming a human pyramid. In this version of the game, three or four players representing plants, the primary producers, form the base, lining up in a single row on their hands and knees. Two or three kids acting as plant-eating animals, the secondary producers, form a row on the backs of the primary producers. At the top of the pyramid, a single player, kneeling on the backs of the secondary producers, represents the meat eaters. As a kid on the sidelines tells a story in which one or more members of a layer are destroyed, the pyramid players act out the results.

Stickler Camouflage

One of the ways animals in the food chain keep from getting gobbled up is by becoming invisible. They don't have to be wizards to do this; they simply need to wear colors that match their backgrounds. Camouflage is what we call this protective coloration. Kids can learn about it firsthand through this game.

Any number of people can play this simple hunt-the-stick game. All you need are *250 flat wooden toothpicks; red, yellow, green, and blue food coloring; a pencil* and *paper;* and *a grassy plot of land.* Before playing, divide the toothpicks into groups of 50 and dye all but one of the groups a different color. Leave the remaining group natural in color. Mix the sticks up well and, while the players aren't looking, scatter the colored sticks or "sticklers" around the plot of grass. Now give the players five minutes to retrieve as many sticks as they can find. When the time is up, tell the

Scientists estimate that in England and Wales each year spiders destroy insects more than equal in weight to the entire human population of that area.
—V. B. Wigglesworth, *The Living World of Insects*

---------------------------------- ✳ ----------------------------------

players to collect the sticks they have found and divide them according to color. Then have the players tally the number of sticks found in each color group. Help them construct a bar graph to show the results. (See How to Chart and Graph Change on page 24.)

If the players found many sticks of one color and few of another, ask them why, and whether they think this would be the case on every plot of land. Then give the players five more minutes to look for the remaining sticks or, if you have time, try the game on a plot with different-colored vegetation.

Create a Critter
This game gives kids a chance to play Mother Nature. In it they devise ingenious ways to adapt animals of their own making to a particular habitat. Before playing Create a Critter, discuss with your kids some of the adaptations real animals have evolved. In the physical world, protective coloration, or camouflage, is only one tool animals use to survive. Many have also evolved special sensory organs and body structures that enable them to detect danger and to capture and eat certain foods. The ladybug larva, for instance, is not only colored brown so it can hide in the shadows underneath leaves, but it is also blessed with a strong set of mandibles or mouth parts to help it devour aphids, mealybugs, and mites.

Any number of people can play this game in any kind of environment. Backyards, vacant lots, streams, beaches, sidewalks, garbage dumps, and sand lots can all provide challenges for your fledgling animal designers. They can also use *virtually any kind of material* for the activity. Potatoes, carrots, paints, toothpicks, sticks, pipe cleaners, cotton, feathers, fabric, plasticene, and cardboard all work well. (You can easily turn this into a trash art project!) To work with these materials, you'll need to gather *scissors, glue, paintbrushes, and the like.* You will also need *index cards,* one for each player, *or paper out of which you can make your own cards.*

After choosing a habitat, develop task cards for each player. Each card will direct the player to create an animal camouflaged to blend into a particular background within the habitat area chosen. A card might read "Create a critter to match the bark of a tree." Others might challenge players to match their critters to a brick wall, a grassy lawn, or a gravel driveway.

Once you have made a set of task cards and gathered materials for creating imaginary animals, discuss with the players the kinds of adaptations they might use in their designs. These may include more than camouflaging strategies. Besides adapting their critters to match the colors, textures, and patterns of the habitat surfaces and backgrounds, kids might invent devices for mobility, body parts that solve specific food-gathering problems, sense organs

for detection of food and danger, and body shapes and coatings for protection against various weather conditions.

Once the players have designed their animals, tell them to place these critters in locations in the habitat they consider most advantageous. The only rule is that the animals must not be hidden. Then conduct an animal hunt. Those best camouflaged should be hardest to find. Once all the animals have been discovered, discuss with the players their reasons for designing their animals the way they did—that is, the survival advantages they thought certain features would provide.

One way to simplify the game is to ask the players to camouflage their animals using only stripes or dots. You might also ask them to use only patterns found on real animals. This simplified version works well with younger children.

For older kids, you can turn Create a Critter into a food chain game by challenging the players to find ways in which their animals can depend on each other for food. One effective way to organize such a game is to compose a set of task cards indicating the kinds of animals to be designed. These might include animals that suck sap from stems, eat leaves, eat plant roots, sip flower nectar, eat plant-eating animals, suck blood from plant-eating animals, and help decompose dead animals. Tell each player to select a card and design an animal to fit the description. Then tell the players to link their animals with other animals that the first can either provide food for or use as food. When they're finished, the players will have formed a food chain.

Yet another variation is to play Create a Critter with competing teams. For this version, you must choose two habitats visually separated from one another. Assign each team to a different habitat. Once the players in each group have constructed and placed their animals on their assigned habitat, tell the teams to switch places and, within a set time limit, to find as many of the other team's critters as possible.

HOW TO GROW A BEAN SPROUT

All you and your kids need to sprout beans are a *handful of bean seeds*, a *jar of cold water*, some *paper towels*, and a *pan or dish*.

1. Soak the beans in the jar of water for about twenty-four hours. To make sure they do not spoil, keep the jar in the refrigerator.

2. Drain off the water and place the beans between damp paper towels in a pan or dish.

3. Store them in a dark place and keep the towels damp.

4. Each day check for changes, using a magnifying lens if you have one. Cut one bean open each day to observe the changes occurring inside. Measure the daily growth of feathery roots and tiny green spikes as they emerge.

Within three or four days you will have sprouted beans, ready for planting or eating.

HOW TO GUIDE AN IMAGINARY JOURNEY

An imaginary journey is like a daydream with a focus. When you prepare to lead your kids on such a journey, think about how you might create conditions conducive to daydreaming. You'll need to find *a quiet spot where your kids can sit or lie down comfortably* so you can lead them into, through, and out of the imaginary journey in as gentle and relaxed a fashion as possible. We found both sitting and lying down work well, although the prone position can lead to snoozing.

If your kids are not used to sitting still with their eyes closed, they may squirm and giggle too much for a full-length imaginary journey. If so, try sneaking in small doses of the experience until they feel comfortable with it. Have them listen to music with their eyes closed or challenge them to guess textures, sounds, or scents while blindfolded. (See Indoor Change Checklist on page 21.)

When you and your kids are ready for an imaginary journey, follow these three simple steps:

1. *Relaxing and grounding.* To enter our imagination fully, we first need to relax our body and free our mind of distracting thoughts. It also helps to feel our connection to the earth before traveling within. When you're ready to begin, ask your kids to find a comfortable position, sitting or lying down, and tell them to take a couple of deep breaths. Ask them as they

breathe out to imagine all the tension flowing out of their bodies with their breath. You might go through body parts, from feet to head, asking them to relax each and to feel themselves sinking into the floor, chair, or earth as they do.

2. *Traveling.* When guiding the journey itself, be sure to speak slowly and calmly, pausing frequently to allow the players to develop their own imaginary scenes. For an example of the wording you might use, see Becoming a Bean Sprout on page 39.

3. *Returning and grounding.* Guiding your kids on their return from an imaginary journey is as important as preparing them for one. If they emerge with a jolt, they might not only have a hard time remembering their inner expedition but also some trouble readjusting to the physical world. Give your kids time to bid farewell to their imaginary world before asking them to return to the pleasant place from which they started. As they return tell them to feel their body pressing into the floor or chair or earth. And let them know they have all the time they need to stretch, yawn, and open their eyes.

To help your kids harvest the rich experiences of their imaginary journey encourage them—without pressuring them—to draw, act out, write, or talk about their inner adventures. Maintain the quiet, open, nonjudgmental mood of the imaginary journey as long as possible.

4. neighborhood ADVENTURES

II. CITY STREETS

THINK OF CITY STREETS AS DIAMONDS in the rough, as places that hold hidden treasures for those willing to scratch the ordinary-looking surface. To help your kids unearth your city's treasure, organize city streets treasure hunts or conduct surveys of everything from bumperstickers to bumblebees. This chapter offers suggestions that you can add to or adapt to any size or age group in any city neighborhood.

Except for the occasional horse, the largest animals you and your kids will find on your urban safaris are the two-legged variety. These creatures built the cities and towns and often think they are the only ones living there. Just as the previous chapter helped you explore plants and wildlife, this one and the following chapter provide games, surveys, and suggestions for investigating the human life in your neighborhood.

The Three-Story Street Games in this chapter parallel those in the previous one but focus on the built environment. By playing both sets of games, your kids will

**Can you tell what time of day it is by
street sounds alone?**

———————————— ✱ ————————————

be able to compare the various ways people, plants, and
non-two-legged animals find shelter, obtain energy, and develop the means to move around.

We include four survey projects in this chap-
ter—covering bumperstickers, street life, traffic, and recreation—as examples. Develop your own questionnaires. Ask
your kids what they want to count or study. Teenagers as
well as very young children can have fun counting things on
their neighborhood streets. Both kids and grownups might
be surprised at what these surveys reveal. If you have the
time and interest, you and your coexplorers can expand
most of these investigations into long-range projects, as
challenging as you wish.

TREASURE HUNTS, OR THINGS TO FIND
Treasure hunts have no right answers. Five people might
find five different things they consider humorous, and all of
these people would be right. In these games, the more different answers players come up with the better.

If you're playing with a group, you might divide up the treasure hunt items lottery-fashion. Write each
item on a slip of paper, put the slips in a box or basket, and
let each player draw one or two or however many you have
to go around. You can play this in teams, with a member
from each team reporting the group's finds after the walk.

To help you tailor a treasure hunt to various
age groups, we've divided hunt suggestions into two lists.
One, the advanced list, is more difficult and abstract than the

———————————— ✱ ————————————

**Eighteen bicycles can be parked in the
space occupied by one automobile.
Thirty can travel in the space required
by one moving automobile.**
—Urban Bikeway Design Collaborative, *Cyclateral Thinking*

other, the starter list. If you're exploring with very young children, you can develop an even simpler, more concrete list with items such as "something red" or "something round."

Treasure hunts make excellent travel games for those times when you and your kids explore beyond your neighborhood. They help keep kids alert and interested in their surroundings on bus, train, and automobile rides.

We've adapted the following two treasure hunt lists, the list of Things to Count (page 70), and the Bumpersticker Survey (page 71) from games and lists in W. Ron Jones's Deschool Primer No. 3: *Your City Has Been Kidnapped.*

THINGS TO FIND (Starter List)
- **something humorous**
- **something like you**
- **a sign of caring**
- **a hiding place**
- **a sign of carelessness**
- **something precious**
- **a monster**
- **something odorless**
- **something you can reuse**
- **something friendly**
- **something that gives you the creeps**
- **something wasteful**
- **an immovable object**
- **something scary**

What kind of power travels through the utility lines? Where does it come from? Are other sources of power available that can do the same jobs?

———————————— * ————————————

THINGS TO FIND (Advanced List)
- **something that can't be photographed**
- **a relic of the past**
- **a symbol of strength**
- **a sign of the times**
- **a message**
- **something that won't be here tomorrow**
- **a sign of hope**
- **a warning or threat**
- **something in disguise**
- **an omen of the future**
- **a sign of fear**
- **a boundary**

SURVEYS, OR THINGS TO COUNT

Surveys tend to be more straightforward than treasure hunts. To make a survey you simply count all the items you can find that belong to a given category of items—for instance, all the telephone poles in a two-block area. The kinds of items you find depend upon the kind of area you are exploring.

Notice which items in the following list of Things to Count apply to your neighborhood and which do not. What does this say about your neighborhood? Make up your own list or add items to the following.

THINGS TO COUNT

- flower beds
- vegetable gardens
- public telephones
- street lights
- birds
- bus stops
- vacant lots
- fenced yards
- unfenced yards
- burglar alarms
- animals other than birds
- television antennas
- swings
- public trash cans
- trees
- laundromats
- broken windows
- manhole covers
- churches
- public restrooms
- hedges
- fast-food outlets
- flat tires
- fire hydrants
- parks

SURVEY PROJECTS: MORE THAN FACTS AND FIGURES

Sometimes counting isn't enough. Simply counting the bumperstickers in your neighborhood, for instance, doesn't tell you nearly as much about the beliefs, values, and opinions of your neighbors as would a survey that included content

---

BUMPERSTICKER SURVEY

1. Choose a three-block area in your neighborhood. How many cars are parked here? _____ How many of these sport bumperstickers? _____ _____ What percentage of the total is this? _____

2. How many of the bumperstickers are humorous? _____ Political? _____ _____ Religious? _____ Folksy? _____ Nonsensical? __ _____ Other? _____

3. On the basis of their bumperstickers, how would you describe your neighbors? Are they serious? Silly? Environmentally concerned? Politically active? Apathetic? Opinionated? Optimistic? Pessimistic? Other? (Circle as many as apply and write in other words that describe your neighbors.)

4. What about the cars without bumperstickers? What do these say about their owners?

5. List three other means your neighbors use to make public announcements of their opinions, beliefs, values, and attitudes. Check telephone poles, walls, windows, t-shirts, and hats for messages.

as well as quantity. Are these people trying to save the world or to simply have a nice day? The answer may lie in the messages on their bumperstickers.

The following four sets of tasks and questions can help you and your kids design four surveys in your neighborhood that involve more than counting. We present the first as a sample worksheet and the other three as sets of questions you may use to develop your own worksheets.

You can turn the following three sets of survey questions into worksheets tailored to your neighborhood, or you and your kids can develop your own surveys using these as examples.

STREET LIFE SURVEY

- **How are the streets in your neighborhood used and by whom? Do kids play in the streets? Do grownups walk their dogs, jog, or gossip there? How about cats, dogs, and birds?**

- **Are your neighborhood streets safe for children and other living things? Do old people feel comfortable here? Can cats and dogs roam on the streets without fear?**

- **Survey the street life in your neighborhood at different hours of the day. How does it change? When are the kids out most? The grownups? The four-footed and winged creatures?**

- **How many different racial and ethnic groups share your neighborhood streets? Does your neighborhood have an ethnic flavor to it? Do many old people live there? Families? Single people?**

NEIGHBORHOOD TRAFFIC SURVEY

- Survey the traffic on your neighborhood streets at different times of day. Which kinds predominate? Auto? Bus? Motorcycle? Bicycle? Two-footed? Four-footed? Winged?

- Survey the traffic at the busiest intersection in your neighborhood at different times of day. Count the motorcycles, bicycles, and pedestrians rushing by as well as the cars. Which kind predominates? Which is least common? What if these figures were reversed? How might your neighborhood be different?

- What kinds of changes might increase the traffic flow in your neighborhood? What kinds might decrease it?

- How many different kinds of traffic signals, signs, and markings can you find in your neighborhood? How well do they control the traffic? Imagine your streets without these. What might the traffic be like? Can you figure out any different ways to control traffic?

- What are the side effects of automobile traffic in your neighborhood? How does it affect the quality of the environment? The patterns of street life? The health of the residents, human and nonhuman?

- Conduct a poll to find out how the people in your neighborhood feel about its traffic. What do they consider its benefits? In what ways would they like it to change?

NEIGHBORHOOD RECREATION SURVEY

- Where do the kids in your neighborhood play? The grownups? What games and sports do they prefer?

- In how many different ways do people use the streets for games and sports? Which of these work best on the streets?

- How many public parks and recreation facilities can you find in your neighborhood? Do you have any softball diamonds? Soccer fields? Basketball or tennis courts? Swimming pools or gymnasiums? What percentage of neighborhood space is devoted to these?

- Who uses the public parks and facilities? Young people? Old people? Boys? Girls? How many different kinds of racial or ethnic groups use them? When are the parks and facilities most crowded?

- Are the parks and facilities safe for everybody? Do some people or groups feel more comfortable using them than others?

- If you could redesign your neighborhood's streets and open space for recreation, what changes would you make? What is your wildest fantasy? Your most practical fantasy?

- Conduct a poll to find out what other people in your neighborhood think about its parks, playgrounds, and other recreational facilities.

THREE-STORY STREET GAMES FOR THE BUILT ENVIRONMENT

As with the other city street games, this one works best if you imagine yourself an alien who has just stepped off an interplanetary ship. You may discover that, even as a human, you don't know what functions the bewildering array of cables, poles, antennas, and sidewalk markers perform.

If six or more of you play this game, you might divide into three teams. Ask each team to explore a different level and share its findings with the others.

WHAT'S UNDERFOOT?

1. Look down at the ground. What do you see? List or draw eight things. Place a check (√) next to those that are alive.

2. How much of the soil in this block is covered with concrete or asphalt? (Circle one.)

   one quarter / half / three quarters / other: _____

3. Can you find any markings on the streets, curbs, or sidewalks? Any special colors? Draw any markings you find and next to the drawings write what you think they mean.

4. Look for manhole covers and other metal or concrete covers and markers on the sidewalk or street. List or draw the covers you find. Beside each item write what you think lurks beneath it.

5. Inspect the trash in and around the street. List three or more kinds. What clues do these give you about the neighborhood? List three or more clues.

Do you think soil that is covered by asphalt or concrete is different from soil that is not covered? How might you find out?

────────────── ✳ ──────────────

────────────── ✳ ──────────────

In Santiago, Chile, traffic has been limited on certain streets to make room for playing courts, communal gardens, and chess and domino tables.

---

*

Plants purify the air, removing carbon dioxide and emitting oxygen. But along a busy highway, the green belt on both sides would have to be a half mile wide to reduce air pollution to one part per 3,000, the standard for human health.

—*Gardens for All News*

WHAT'S AT EYE LEVEL?

1. Look around at eye level. What kinds of things do you see? List or draw eight of these. Put a check (✓) beside anything that is living. Put two checks (✓ ✓) beside anything that is an animal. (Don't forget the two-legged variety.)

2. Choose one house or building to observe. Can you find signs of any creatures other than people who live here? _____ List three of them.

3. Imagine you are a mouse. Where might you find a place to live in this building?

4. Notice and feel the different textures at eye level. Make crayon rubbings of two tree trunk textures and two building textures.

5. How many cars and trucks can you see from where you are standing? _____

How many garages and driveways? _____ How much space on this block do you think cars take up, including the streets, garages, and driveways they need? (Circle one.) one quarter / half / three quarters / other: _____

6. Wave a magic wand and turn all the cars and trucks into airplanes. List three ways this block would be different if the residents flew airplanes instead of drove cars.

7. Wave your magic wand again and turn all the cars and trucks you see here into bicycles. List three ways the block would be different if bicycling and walking were the only forms of transportation.

WHAT'S OVERHEAD?

1. Look above your head. What things can you see at roof- and treetop level? List or draw eight of these. Put a check (√) beside any that can send or receive messages.

2. Notice the telephone poles and the lines that run from these poles into the houses. How many houses are connected to each pole? _____

3. What do the lines strung between the poles and the houses do besides carry telephone messages?

4. How many birds can you count on the telephone lines, television antennas, and rooftops? _____

5. Imagine that all the poles and lines on your block blew down in a gale. How would your life be different? Describe three or more ways.

HOW TO MAKE A BOARD GAME, OR WHO NEEDS PARKER BROS. ANYWAY?

Lots of kids play board games, but few make their own. Besides being fun, easy to construct, and a great way to spend a rainy afternoon, these games can help kids relive the adventures of a city expedition.

The subject matter of the board game is limited only by the imagination of the designers. Kids can create board games about the adventures in the life of a city cat, the plant and insect interactions in a vacant lot, or the opportunities and obstacles involved in developing their own neighborhood

playground. Anything you and your kids have explored in the city can be given a starring role in a board game.

The board game described and illustrated here is a simple one. To make it you need a *manila file folder,* a *pen or a set of color pens, one jumbo paperclip, one metal brad,* and *small household items to use as counters.* Once you and your kids have chosen a topic for your game, you can decide what kinds of pictures to draw in the squares. If several of you are illustrating a single board game, you might draw your pictures on separate sheets of paper, then cut them out and paste them on the squares of the board.

In the sections of the spinner circle, write commands that refer to specific moves on the board, such as "Move forward three squares" or "Return to 'start.'" If you have made one or more sets of cards for your game, be sure to include commands in the spinner circle referring to these. A typical command would be "Choose a card from the reward deck."

You might make one deck including both reward and penalty cards or separate decks for each. If you create both a reward and a penalty deck, mark the backs of the cards in each set "Reward" or "Penalty." To further distinguish them, make each set of cards out of a different color paper. If you and your kids want to make an even more elaborate game, study commercial board games and borrow features from them.

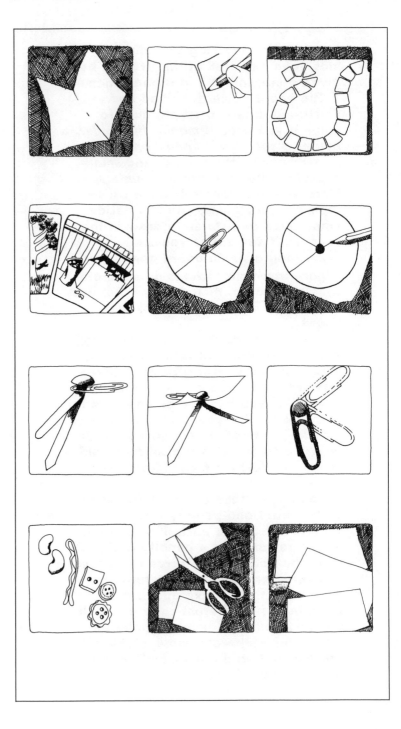

1. Open a manila file folder.
2. On the inside draw a row of large squares.
3. Make the row as crooked as you like.
4. In each square draw a picture of something in your neighborhood or city.
5. In an empty corner make a spinner like this one.
6. First, draw a circle with lines across it. Then, in each section write a command.
7. Thread the legs of a large brad through one end of a jumbo paperclip.
8. Poke a hole in the center of the circle and push the brad legs through it.
9. Adjust the brad so the paperclip can spin.
10. Gather beans, buttons, bobby pins, or other items for counters.
11. Cut one or more sets of cards from heavy paper. (Optional)
12. Write a command on each card. (Optional)

$*$

The average bicyclist can travel for 100 miles on the energy equivalent of one gallon of gasoline, achieving fuel mileage comparable to 1,100 miles per gallon.
—*Co-Evolution Quarterly*

$*$

Green belts in and around cities help stabilize temperatures, while areas that are all asphalt and concrete experience extremes of hot and cold, wet and dry conditions.
—*Gardens for All News*

5. *neighborhood* ADVENTURES

III. CITY PEOPLE

TO LEARN CERTAIN FACTS ABOUT YOUR NEIGHBOR-HOOD AND CITY, you and your kids may need to talk with people directly. This chapter offers tips on conducting interviews and interview-based surveys. It includes theater games for warming up and suggests projects that can put you "on the air"—at least in your imaginations.

INTERVIEWING PEOPLE FOR FUN AND FACTS

The talks you and your kids conduct with people might range from informal conversations with neighbors to street-corner surveys of the general public to formal interviews with experts.

The two examples below will help your coexplorers understand the difference between a public opinion poll—or street-corner survey—and an in-depth interview. In an opinion poll, the researcher asks people at random what they think about an issue. These polls usually consist of a brief list of questions and require no special knowledge on the part of the person being polled. For a formal interview, the researcher seeks out people experienced or knowledgeable in a particular area and digs for facts as well as

opinions. With these, the list of questions tends to be both longer and more specific.

The people you and your kids interview need not have degrees after their names to be considered experts. Experts could include oldtimers who remember what a neighborhood looked like fifty years ago, garbage collectors who can tell you how much trash your neighborhood generates and where it goes after it is picked up, or kids themselves. The children of the neighborhood would be among the best sources of information, for instance, on how well local recreational facilities meet their needs. Are there enough parks, playgrounds, and basketball courts? Do these feel safe? Are they fun to play in? Your list of interview

---

ON-THE-STREET SURVEY

1. Do you live or work in this neighborhood? ☐ Yes ☐ No **If yes, why did you choose this location? If no, what brings you here?** _____

2. What do you like about this neighborhood? _____

3. What do you dislike about this neighborhood? _____

4. What changes do you think would improve this neighborhood? _____

NEIGHBORHOOD SHOPKEEPER INTERVIEW

1. How long have you been in business here? _____

2. Why did you choose this location?

_____

3. Do you, or whoever owns the shop, live in (circle one): This neighborhood? _____ Elsewhere in the city? __ _____ Out of town? _____

4. How many employees live in the neighborhood? _____ Elsewhere in the city? _____ Out of town?

_____

Questions 5 and 6, can be answered by the words "none," "some," or "most."

5. How many of your customers live in the neighborhood? _____

6. How many shop here regularly? _____

_____

7. How many of your products are made or grown:

In the neighborhood? _____

Elsewhere in the city? _____

Out of town but within the state?

_____

Out of state but within the country?

_____

Outside the country? _____

8. What foreign countries, if any, do your products come from? _____

9. Are you in contact with other shops in the neighborhood? _____ If so, in what ways? _____

10. How do you think your shop benefits the neighborhood? _____

11. How do you think your shop creates problems for the neighborhood? _____
_____

12. In what ways would you like to see the neighborhood improved? _____

subjects might include local merchants, police officers, librarians, city council members, and bus drivers.

PREPARING FOR THE INTERVIEW: TIPS AND GAMES

Before you and your kids conduct a survey or interview, you might rehearse what you plan to say. Even simple on-the-street surveys in familiar neighborhoods demand that kids be confident, assertive, articulate, and considerate.

In-depth interviews with experts require more planning than street-corner surveys. For these you usually need to request an appointment. Sometimes this involves writing or telephoning the person you wish to interview. These interviews offer excellent opportunities for your children to learn phone etiquette and proper letter-writing form.

Be sure your coexplorers know that, in requesting an interview, they should identify themselves, tell why they are writing or phoning, explain the purpose of the interview and the amount of time they will need for it, offer several possible meeting times, and ask the person which time is most convenient for him or her.

Remind your children about the importance of arriving on time for the interview and the courtesy of sending a thank-you note to the person interviewed within a week following the session.

Even well-planned questions, polished shoes, and respectful letters of introduction won't guarantee that your budding interviewers won't dissolve into giggles or

**We know that animals camouflage
themselves for protection. Can you
think of any ways people do the same?**

──────────────────── ✳ ────────────────────

suffer an attack of stage fright when they walk into the
mayor's office or introduce themselves to their first pas-
serby. To reduce the chances of these occurrences try some
role playing before you head out the door with your clipboards and questions.

Miming, Moving, and Role Playing

Imagine you are a rookie police officer walking a beat in
your city or town. How do you move your feet? How do you
hold your body? Your arms? Where are you looking? What
are you noticing? What are you wearing? Begin walking as
if you were a police officer on a beat. How do you feel?

Now imagine you are an old woman walking
the same street. How are you moving and holding your
body? What are you noticing? Wearing? Begin walking as if
you were an old woman on the street. How do you feel?

The best people-watchers and interviewers
are those who can develop empathy with other people. In
their imagination, they can step into another person's shoes
and feel what it must be like to be that person.

The miming and mock-interview games
below provide excellent preparation for on-the-street surveys and formal interviews. They help kids loosen up, shed
self-consciousness, and develop a sense of connectedness
with people in a variety of roles and situations. Both are
variations of exercises actors use to help themselves identify with different characters. For each, we give instructions
for how you, as the guide, can direct the players.

Warm-Up Puppet Game

*Stretch first one arm, then the other above
your head, as if you were picking plums
high up in a plum tree. Keep alternating
your stretches. Now, bend your knees*

slightly and fold over at the waist,
dropping your hands to the floor and
hanging limp like a rag doll. Shake your
head from side to side and wiggle your
arms. Now, slowly roll back up, imagining
that a string attached to your head is
pulling you to your full height. Feel
yourself being led around by this string as
if you were a puppet. Now, imagine the
string attached to your chin. You are being
pulled forward, with your chin jutting out
in front of the rest of you. How do you feel
walking this way? If you walked this way
all the time, do you think you would think
and act differently? How would you
behave? How would people respond to
you? Imagine you are a character on the
street walking like this, chin first. Where
are you going? How are you dressed? What
are you thinking about?

Repeat this process, asking the players to imagine the string attached to their stomach, feet, chest, or other parts of their body. Help them find out how many different kinds of characters they can become simply by changing their posture as they walk.

How Many Different People Can You Be?
Now that your prospective interviewers are limbered up and feeling like they have ten personalities instead of one, you can help them practice for their on-the-street surveys. As they continue to mill about, walking as if they had strings attached to different parts of their body, assume the role of on-the-street interviewer. Using an imaginary microphone, ask the kids questions and tell them to respond as they think the characters they are portraying would. You might ask: Who are you? What do you do? How do you like the neighborhood? After five or ten minutes, pass the imaginary mike to the kids and let them take turns acting as interviewer.

If your kids plan to conduct interviews with local experts, use role playing to practice specific interview situations. Begin with the kinds of imagination and mime games described above. If your kids are going to interview oldtimers, ask them to walk, sit, and gesture like them. Then let the kids take turns playing both interviewer and expert. Encourage them in both roles to act out a number of different responses to the same situation.

After the interviews, as a follow-up, repeat the miming and role playing. How are they different from the warm-ups? What new information about their subjects are the kids including now? What stereotypes have been shattered?

HOW TO PRODUCE A MAKE-BELIEVE RADIO OR TV SHOW

You and your kids can improvise a mock radio or television show in an hour or after weeks of planning and research. The show can serve as a simple follow-up for one of your neighborhood expeditions or as a spontaneous rainy-day activity. If you wish, you can turn it into an in-depth research project requiring several neighborhood outings, interviews, and surveys in addition to library work. You might find this project an easy, playful way of introducing kids to public speaking and library research. The only materials you will need are *a few props.* These can be as simple as handlettered signs or as elaborate as microphones, tape recorders, and video cameras.

If you decide to improvise a brief show after a walk around the block, you and your kids can take turns being talk-show hosts or on-the-scene television news reporters. You can interview each other about what you discovered on the day's expedition and report the results of any surveys you conducted.

For those of you who choose to produce a full news program, complete with researched stories, here are six steps for putting together this make-believe media event.

1. *Choose a format and a focus.* Do you want your program to be a special focusing on one issue or geographical area? Or would you rather mimic the format of a regular evening news show and include sports, weather, and human-interest reporting along with the hard news?

2. *Choose roles and tasks.* You're all familiar with the people who present the news on the air, but what about those behind the scenes? In addition to an anchor and several reporters, your news program will need a producer, an editor, a production manager, and possibly other specialists. If you are working with a small group, you can each assume more than one role.

3. *Choose and assign stories.* If you plan to focus on neighborhood news, ask your kids what interests them most about their neighborhood and how they can turn this into news. They might look, for instance, at what the neighborhood's biggest claim to fame or most crying need is, how the neighborhood is changing, what birds vacation there, or who its most famous or eccentric human resident might be. Next, you might help the kids decide how to assign stories. Does the producer make the final decision? Do they draw straws? Or do they try to reach consensus as a group? Let them decide.

4. *Develop a production schedule.* Among other things, your kids will need to gather props, schedule rehearsals, and set deadlines for researching, writing, and editing stories. Help them figure out what needs to be done and how to do it.

5. *Find experts to help.* Find out whether anyone in the group has friends or friends of friends with experience in television or radio production who would be willing to give time to your project. Or call a local station or a nearby college for assistance. If you can, arrange a visit to a local television or radio studio to find out how real television and radio shows are produced.

6. *Do it.* Perform your radio or television news show for your friends, families, neighbors, classmates, or whomever you and your kids can cajole into watching it. It helps to have an audience. If you think the stories you have developed are valuable and interesting, offer them to the nearest radio or television station. Who knows? Your mock electronic media performance might become a real one.

An alternative: Those of you who enjoy reading and writing might consider breaking into the print media. Why not publish your own neighborhood newspaper? Follow the same steps listed above, but gear your final product to the printed rather than the spoken word. You can turn your make-believe newspaper into a real one simply by duplicating copies and passing them out.

6. *heading* DOWNTOWN

JOURNEYING DOWNTOWN, ESPECIALLY TO the financial district of a large city, can be as alien an adventure for your kids as an expedition to the heart of a forest. A sense of seriousness and mystery emanates from this domain of grownups. Wind roars through the cool, dark canyons created by the rows of tall buildings. Crowds of gray-suited men and women, looking not unlike coveys of quail, scurry through guarded entries to perform unknown tasks behind closed doors.

For children, a trip downtown can resemble a visit to a foreign country. Each such place has its own

**If you could turn all the flat rooftops in
your city into gardens, how many acres
of green space would you add to your
city?**

———————————— * ————————————

particular rules, strange language, special dress, and unfamiliar pace. Like a visit abroad or to the woods, a trip to
a city's business district can wake up a child's mind and
senses and cast a fresh light on his or her familiar environment back home.

Even small cities hold their mysteries. How
many kids—or grownups, for that matter—know what goes
on behind the familiar facades of banks, business offices,
bus stations, factories, and municipal utility plants? Most of
us have only a vague idea how many people, jobs, kilowatts
of electricity, and barrels of oil are needed to make the life
of a city, even a small city, possible.

In this chapter you will find ways to explore
the mysteries of your city's downtown area. What do people
do there? How do they get there? Why are they in such a
hurry? What other creatures live downtown? How do the
mice and sparrows, sycamores and marigolds survive?
Where do the building materials come from? What's going
on underground? The activities suggested here include not
only things to do once you arrive downtown but games to
play on your way, whether you travel by car, train, or bus.

Although these activities have been de-
signed for the downtown area of a major city, you can adapt
them for use in small cities or in parts of town other than
the business district. You might find the industrial sector of
your town a more mysterious place to explore with kids
than the downtown area.

Once you've investigated your city's busi-
ness or industrial district, try traveling out of town to a
nearby woods, beach, or farm district. As paradoxical as it
may sound, taking such a trip with kids can be an effective
way of helping them better understand the city.

BEFORE SETTING OUT: TOOLS, RULES, AND TIPS

Whatever unfamiliar urban terrain you choose to explore, you will find the skills your kids acquired on your neighborhood expeditions—how to conduct treasure hunts, surveys, interviews and such—will serve them well on these trips beyond the neighborhood. But you might discover that these unfamiliar environments either overwhelm or over-stimulate your child friends. The kids might clam up when it comes time to conduct an interview, or they might create such a commotion walking down a street or through a building that they change the environment they are supposed to be observing.

One way we found to help kids both overcome their shyness and keep a rein on their exuberance was to turn the expedition into a game of sleuthing. We asked kids to imagine they were private eyes, special investigators commissioned to observe without being observed. We told them to picture themselves dressed in imaginary trench coats with make-believe hats pulled low over their eyes and notebooks in hand. Then we gave them their assignment: they were to slip into the central city unseen to collect the facts and solve the mysteries of how a busy metropolis functions. We reminded them that they need not always stay in the background. Even detectives and private investigators identify themselves and interview people when appropriate.

Before setting off for unfamiliar territory, we discussed the unwritten rules we might find downtown. We all know about the written rules, the signals that tell us to stop or go and the signs that warn us about littering, curbing our dogs, and trespassing. But what about the rules that aren't written down? What kinds of behavior would be out of place even if no signs or city laws prohibit them? This kind of discussion not only prepares kids for what will be expected of them in an unfamiliar and adult domain, it also provides them with an intriguing mystery to investigate.

Keep in mind that exploring the downtown or industrial sectors of your city also means investigating birds, flowers, spiders, and trees—all of which can be found even in the most heavily developed sections of town by those who look closely enough. In Wild Places (page 32), we told how in a weedy parking lot in San Francisco's financial district, group after group of children made marvelous discoveries about insect eggs, bird nests, and green growing things. In other downtown forays, these and other groups discovered secret gardens on rooftops as well as no end of spiders, snails, and beetles amid the bushes and trees that grew in the landscaping around office buildings.

But these represent only the most obvious forms of nature in a built environment. Not so obvious are the riverbeds, alpine peaks, and redwood forests transformed into concrete sidewalks, granite sidings, and wooden doors and window frames. Everything in the city originates in nature. Becoming aware of this helps us understand the bonds between the city and the natural world and the impact they have on each other. At the end of this section, along with tips on investigating the history of your city, we provide suggestions for designing and conducting nature walks through your city's commercial areas.

ON YOUR WAY
Part of the fun of heading downtown is getting there. Unless you happen to live downtown, you and the kids with whom you're exploring will pass through a cross-section of the city on your way from your residential neighborhood to your downtown destination. As passengers in a car, bus, or train, you will be in an excellent position to begin sleuthing. You can view your surroundings and your fellow passengers without drawing attention to yourself. If you're traveling by public transportation, playing private eye with your kids will focus their attention on the world outside and lessen the chances you'll have to play disciplinarian. Moreover, your kids will have a chance to see a slice of the city that may be unfamiliar: various subcultures of people, styles of architecture, and natural and built environments.

We found the kinds of treasure hunts we described in the sections on change and city streets (pages 22

PEOPLE-WATCHING ON THE BUS

1. Count the people of different ages riding this bus. How many old people? _____ Infants? _____
Children under thirteen? _____
Teenagers? _____ Others? _____

2. Count the people of different racial and ethnic backgrounds riding this bus. How many Asians? _____
Blacks? _____ Whites? _____
_____ Hispanics? _____ Native Americans? _____ Others? _____

3. Can you hear any dialects or foreign languages being spoken? _____
If so, which ones? _____

4. At what streets do most people board the bus? _____ Why do you think this is so? _____

5. At what streets do most people leave the bus? _____ Why do you think this is so? _____

6. How are people behaving on the bus? They are (circle as many as apply):

    talking / sleeping / reading / singing / listening to the radio / staring out the window / eating / smoking.

7. Do you see any rules for behavior written on the bus? What are they? __

8. Can you figure out the unwritten rules of bus behavior? If so, what are they? _____

9. Do you notice anyone breaking the rules? _____ If so, which ones?

_____

*

Bicycles and pedicabs in Bangkok and Hong Kong move more quickly than buses and cars do in New York or Boston.
—Urban Bikeway Design Collaborative, *Cyclateral Thinking*

and 68) worked well as travel games. Before heading out, ask each kid to choose several items to look for. We also encourage kids to unobtrusively people-watch on the bus. Here's a sample worksheet you can use as is or adapt to your kids' reading level and the particular bus route you plan to take.

WHEN YOU ARRIVE
Once you arrive downtown, you can carry out your private-eye investigations in any number of ways. You can study the people, the buildings, or the patterns of city life. You can search for hidden gardens and birds' nests or concentrate on the built environment. You can stay in the background, observing silently, or assert yourselves by taking polls and conducting interviews.

In our trips to the San Francisco financial district with kids, we found that friendly assertiveness and a bit of luck opened many unlikely doors. On one excursion with thirty fifth-graders, we gained entry—simply by asking permission—to a garden we had spied on the roof of a bank building. The garden happened to be outside the bank president's penthouse office. Sensing this was no ordinary opportunity and awed by the elegant, hushed environment, the children fell quite silent as they tiptoed out to the plant-filled rooftop terrace for a look at nature in the financial district.

In another unplanned encounter with nature, we and a group of eight-year-olds discovered trees that rained honey on Montgomery Street, San Francisco's counterpart to Wall Street in New York. We were about to enter the revolving doors of the Transamerica Pyramid Building when we noticed a row of tall, skinny eucalyptus trees festooned with tufts of brilliant red flowers. We knew that a cup filled with drops of nectar nestled deep inside the stamen fur of each flower, ready to be sipped by a passing bee or hummingbird.

We decided to pretend, at least for a moment, that we were hummingbirds and bees. As we clustered around the trunk of one of the trees, the tallest of us shook the branches filled with red flowers. Droplets of sweet

STREET-CORNER PEOPLE WATCHING

1. How are people working here? List all the jobs you see people performing at or near this street corner.

2. How are people getting around? List or draw the kinds of transportation you see people using here.

   Which kind is predominant? _____
   Which appears to be fastest? _____
   Which kinds do not use gasoline? __
   _____

3. What are the written rules here? List the signs or symbols that tell people what to do.

4. What are the unwritten rules here? List as many of these as you can figure out.

5. Can you find any rule-breakers? _____ _____ If so, list the rules they are breaking.

   _____
   _____

liquid rained down on our tongues and hands and soon even the pavement was splotched with wetness. We all closed our eyes to better taste the fragrant eucalyptus nectar.

Not all our activities downtown are unplanned. We bring worksheets along and call ahead to make arrangements to visit certain buildings. Here we provide three sample worksheets. Of the first two, one focuses on people, the other on buildings. We usually people-watch as soon as we step off the bus or streetcar, at the busy intersection of Market and Montgomery streets. Then we head for a block with a variety of impressive buildings to conduct our Banks and Other Buildings activity.

We design many of our downtown worksheets for particular sites we plan to visit. The Transamerica Pyramid Building is always a favorite. From here kids can see three bridges, three islands, several rooftop gardens, and some of the most historic blocks in San Francisco. Because the Pyramid also offers them a bird's-eye view of such things as traffic flow, building patterns, and geographical features, we usually ask kids questions relating to these. We often ask them to estimate the percentage of city space devoted to cars, or to figure out alternative uses for rooftops. You and your kids might search out the highest viewpoint you can find in your city and design some bird's-eye-view quizzes for your trip there.

SIZING UP AN ENVIRONMENT
We found this environment quiz in poster form in Ron Jones's Deschool Primer Series (see bibliography). We converted it to a worksheet and used it to explore our responses to everything from a city park to a downtown highrise.

On one of our trips to San Francisco's financial district, this time with a group of teenagers, we applied the quiz to the Federal Reserve Building, then located at the corner of Sansome and Clay streets. An awesome structure, this building symbolizes financial power and evoked in us a combination of fear and awe.

All of us—kids and grownups alike—felt small and insignificant as we climbed the broad stone steps to the entrance, passed between fifty-foot-high columns, and pushed through a massive set of ornamental metal doors.

───────────── ＊ ─────────────

Does your city have a Chinatown, a Little Italy or other ethnic districts? If so, find out how they developed and how they contribute to your city's culture.

BANKS AND OTHER BUILDINGS

1. How many stories is the tallest building you can see from here? _____ _____

2. Which building looks friendliest? (List its name or address.) _____
Most dignified? _____ **Least inviting?** _____ **Most likely to win a building beauty contest?** _____ _____

3. If you were to name three of the above buildings, what would you name them? _____ **Draw your favorite of these.**

4. Out of what material(s) is the facade of your favorite building made? _____ _____

5. Count the different types of building materials used for the facades of buildings in this block. How many can you see? _____ **List the types of materials.**

6. Which of the buildings you can see from here is oldest? _____
Newest? _____ **How can you tell? List the clues.**

7. What kinds of buildings do you not see here? Name three.

———————————————— ✳ ————————————————

The hole excavated for the foundation of the Bank of America Building, one of San Francisco's tallest, would take one person shoveling dirt eight hours a day fifty-one years to fill in again.
—Bank of America World Headquarters Building Fact Sheet, 1975

We immediately sensed that we were being watched. We turned around, swept the wall with our eyes and found ourselves looking down the muzzle of a rifle. Halfway up the wall in an enclosed mezzanine, a guard behind bulletproof glass aimed the gun in our direction. Its muzzle pointed through a sight hole in the window. The hair raised on our necks, our hearts beat faster, we caught our breath, but for several long seconds we could not take our eyes off that rifle.

This place both frightened and fascinated us. What could be so valuable that it required such security measures? What do the guards and guns say about the role of money in our culture? Whose money are they guarding? Where does it go when it leaves this building? Who makes these decisions? Question after question pushed its way into our heads, but we didn't stay for answers. We introduced ourselves to the staff, filled out our worksheets and quickly left. We breathed freely again once we reached the sunlight outside. We imagined the guards, clerks, and managers inside were breathing more freely also now that our group of twenty-five curious teenagers and teachers were safely out the door.

Try this test in two or three different kinds of environments and compare your answers. In what kinds of places do you feel relaxed? Powerful? Alert? Scared? Insignificant? Playful? If you were an architect or a planner, how would you design a school building? A park? A city?

WHEN YOU RETURN

Learning about your city's downtown doesn't end when you board the bus to return from your trip. Back at home or school, you and your kids can spend hours, even weeks, following up on your downtown explorations. If you have explored your neighborhood using the activities in this book, you already have a variety of tools and skills for conducting your downtown follow-up. You can make graphs, charts, and maps; develop your own downtown board game; try miming, moving, and role playing; or take

HOW WOULD YOU DESCRIBE THIS ENVIRONMENT?

1. The entrance to _____ is (circle one):

> inviting / threatening / intriguing / confusing / other: _____

2. The dominant color is: _____

3. The dominant sound is: _____

4. The most numerous objects I see in this environment are: _____

5. The purpose of this environment appears to be: _____

6. Something out of place in this environment is: _____

7. Something I would like to add to this environment is: _____

8. The funny thing about this environment is: _____

9. If I were to describe this environment according to one-word definitions, I would characterize it as (circle one in each pair):

> hard/soft old/new open/closed
> big/little calming/threatening
> female/male just/unjust
> safe/dangerous have/have not
> black/white alive/dead

10. This environment makes me feel:

_____
_____

11. A suitable slogan for this environment is:

_____
_____
_____

one another on imaginary trips back in time or forward into the future.

Here are seven suggestions for downtown follow-up activities:

1. Make a large map of the downtown area you visited and mark the landmarks you found—secret gardens, tall buildings, prime people-watching spots, and such.

2. Investigate the history of your city's downtown area and of the buildings you explored. (See How to Trace Your City's History on page 112.)

3. Use fantasy, mime, and role playing to imagine and express how downtown city life must feel for people of different ages and backgrounds and in various types of work. What kinds of challenges does downtown pose for an old person? A mother with children? A foreigner who doesn't speak the language? A disabled person? What must it feel like to work downtown as a bus driver? A police officer? An insurance executive? A stockbroker? A secretary?

4. Use your imagination to explore what it might be like to be a bus, a building, or a bird downtown.

5. Develop science fiction scenarios— both reasonable and outlandish—about the downtown of the future. What if computers and robots took over most of the jobs? What if all the machines, facilities, services, and systems gradually broke down? What if people

learned to communicate telepathically? What if automobiles and air conditioners were banned?

6. Develop a walker's guide to the downtown area, complete with the history, natural features, unusual buildings, and unwritten rules you found. (See How to Plan a Nature Walk Through Your City's Downtown on page 116.)

7. Lead other groups—a gathering of neighbors, a group of schoolmates, the local Kiwanis Club—on tours of the downtown area.

HEADING OUT OF TOWN

If you have a chance to take your kids out of town, do it. Not only can a visit to the countryside develop camaraderie and provide fun, adventure, and a breath of fresh air, it can also give kids a new perspective on the city and a deeper understanding of its place in the larger environment.

We learned this during our work with a group of fourteen-year-olds from San Francisco's Mission District. All twenty-five of these junior high school kids were educationally disadvantaged in one way or another. Either they had just arrived in the United States and could barely speak English, or they had never learned to read or write

*

Two grade-school classes, one in New York's Harlem, the other in Vermont, conducted a city-country exchange, trading scrapbooks and reports on their environmental projects. At the end of the year, the students visited each other's communities.

**An acre's worth of soil in a vacant lot
can contain up to one ton of fungi,
several tons of bacteria, 200 pounds of
protozoa (one-celled animals), 100
pounds of algae, and 100 pounds of
yeasts. Soil is thus the highest
concentration of life power on earth.**
—*The Living World of Nature*

---------------------------------- ✳ ----------------------------------

above fourth-grade level, or they had been kicked out of every other class for misconduct. Some were introverted and quiet, others boisterous and bullying. All were having trouble making it.

Our task was to help these inner-city kids learn about environments. We had eight days in which to do it, and the job proved to be one of our toughest and most memorable teaching experiences.

We decided to make the project a study in contrasts, starting with the highly urbanized areas in which we lived and ending with a natural setting 150 miles to the north. We hoped this opportunity to study a wide range of environments, including several new to the students, would broaden their world and loosen static images they might have of their urban neighborhoods. The trips we designed started with a plunge into San Francisco's highrise financial district and ended with three days at Jughandle Creek Ecological Reserve near Mendocino, California. The slice of coastal land preserved at Jughandle Creek includes beach, meadows, and a rare pygmy forest, as well as an old farmhouse now used as a hostel and nature study center.

To our surprise, the streetwise kids marched into San Francisco's financial district with glee but urged retreat when faced with the possibility of a trip to the country. They warned of bears, dark nights, strangers, and two and a half days without television. The motley handful of kids who bravely chose to go on the Jughandle trip instead found redwood forests, red-tailed hawks, and an easy companionship they never experienced in the classroom. Even

**Once you've researched the history of
your city's street names, design a street
names crossword puzzle to stump your
friends and neighbors.**

✻

---

the two girls who chose to stay inside most of the time,
straightening and cleaning the farmhouse, appeared to develop a new appreciation of nature. On the trip home, they
were the first to point out the natural features of the city.
"Hey, look at those birds!" they exclaimed as we drove past
Golden Gate Park. "And check out those trees." The two
seemed to be seeing the birds, trees, and green spaces of
their city for the first time.

We decided that if even minimal exposure to
the countryside could help these kids view the city with
fresh eyes, the trips out of town were worth the effort.

Where to Look
You might be surprised at what is available within a hun-
dred-mile radius of your city or town. Check with the chamber of commerce, your visitor center, the county or state
parks department, your auto club, or the local library. Look
for nature study centers or farms or dairies that conduct
tours. Or find a state or county park that provides self-
guided nature trails. Talk with park rangers. You might find
one willing to design a special tour for you and your kids.

✻

**In downtown San Francisco the facades
of the I. Magnin Co., the Hibernia
Bank, the Pacific Mutual Life Building,
and the State Office Building are made
of, respectively, marble from Vermont,
quartz and feldspar from the
Sacramento Valley, orthoclase from
Norway, and granite from Sweden.**
—*The Walker's Guide to the Geology of San Francisco*

HOW TO TRACE YOUR CITY'S HISTORY

The history of a place is written in its hills and valleys, waterways, and vegetation as well as in books about the area. Regard your city as a fact of nature. Find out where ancient streams still run and what, if any, of its native vegetation remains. By studying old maps and early artistic renderings, reconstruct the natural geography of the place, complete with watershed and wildlife.

Begin by asking questions. Then figure out how to find the answers. You'll be surprised at the wealth of resources in your own backyard. Here are examples of questions you and your kids can investigate:

1. What natural features and resources led people to choose this site for a home?
Activities. Take walking trips around your city looking for signs of its ancient streams and native vegetation. Record these on a map. Now make a map of how you imagine this land looked before a city was built on it.
Resources. City planning, parks and recreation, and municipal utility departments; local museums, nature centers, or historical societies; local chapters of environmental groups; public or college libraries.

2. How did early settlers from other countries and, before them, native peoples find food, water, and shelter in what is now your city?
Activities. Visit museums or parks that feature displays of early life in your

area. Talk with people who are studying this early life. Ask native people and the descendents of early settlers to tell you stories that have been passed down about life in this area. Prepare the kinds of meals settlers and native people might have eaten. Fashion the kinds of tools they used and clothes they wore.
*Resources.*Local parks and museums; ethnic organizations; historians, anthropologists, and librarians at a nearby college or university; local historical societies; public libraries.

3. How has life in your city changed over the past hundred years?
*Activities.*Visit old buildings and historical landmarks in your city. Look for traces of life as it used to be. Can you find a hitching post? Old advertisements painted on the sides of buildings? The remnants of streetcar tracks no longer in use? Conduct an oral history project: talk with and record the stories of oldtimers. Collect old photos and make a scrapbook or slide show of your city's or neighborhood's history.
*Resources.*Parents, grandparents, neighbors, shopkeepers, and well-known oldtimers; city planning, public works, and county records departments; school and public libraries; local historical societies.

Learning from Diaries, Letters, and Storytellers
When we studied San Francisco's past with ten-to-twelve-year-olds, we were fortunate to have access to the

handwritten memoirs of a man who, at age fourteen, had jumped ship in San Francisco Bay and joined the gold rush in the 1850s. We passed around copies of the man's story in the classroom. The kids were fascinated not only by this person's plainly worded descriptions of his daily life and adventures but also by his spidery handwriting and occasional misspellings. The document brought the gold rush to life for them.

The archivist for the San Francisco Public Library suggests that children not only read other people's diaries of life in the city but that they keep records of their own. Such diary keeping, she explains, helps kids realize that the times through which they are living will be history in a few years. They can look upon these records of daily life as treasures that they can later pass on to their own children and grandchildren.

Kids might also look at copies of local newspapers from times past. These, along with diaries and letters, can provide a lively glimpse into the history of their city.

Even more dramatic and appealing than these written sources of history are people themselves telling stories of times past. More and more libraries are collecting the taped stories of oldtimers, and increasing numbers of librarians are becoming skilled in oral history. Ask your librarians whether they can give you and your kids pointers on how to conduct an oral history project. They may ask you, in turn, to add the information you collect to the library archives.

Learning from Street Names

Ever wonder where streets get their names? You might play a game with your kids of seeing how much you can learn about your city from street names alone, kind of a city streets version of Trivial Pursuit.

To get started, you may need to check a few history books out of your local library or collect copies of old city maps. Imagine yourselves archaeologists hundreds of years from now. You're trying to figure out how this city grew and changed over the years, and the only clues you have are street names.

Do street names give any indication of which parts of town were built first or which buildings are the oldest? Did any street names change over the years? If so, what do the changes reveal? What do street names say about who lived in the city in years past? Who built it? What activities went on? What streets were most important? What kinds of trees and other natural features were prominent?

HOW TO PLAN A NATURE WALK THROUGH YOUR CITY'S DOWNTOWN

Many people consider a city's downtown area anything but natural. But that's usually because they have a narrow definition of nature. Our favorite nature walk takes participants through the center of San Francisco's highrise financial district. As we lead kids and grownups through the district's windswept corridors, we like to surprise them by pointing out the Italian Alps cut and polished into granite slabs on bank facades, the streambeds of the Sierra foothills hardened into concrete sidewalks beneath our feet, and the redwood forests toppled and planed into the decks and doorways of dining spots.

As we amble down Montgomery Street, the so-called Wall Street of the West, we amaze our listeners by informing them that they are walking on the not-so-ancient shoreline of San Francisco Bay. Until the 1850s, we remind them, what is now Montgomery Street formed the eastern edge of the city. Beyond it lay the bay, crowded, in its gold rush heyday, with tall-masted schooners, most of which never left port because their crew members had fled to the gold fields. Instead, these graceful ships became part of the bayfill upon which today's banks and corporate headquarters rest. Those in our groups who look carefully find a faint blue line painted on a section of Montgomery Street and a bronze plaque embedded in the sidewalk at the corner of Battery and Market streets, both denoting the site of the former bay shore. The markers remind our tour members and other passersby that beneath their feet and among what are now pilings of concrete and steel the tides used to rise and fall. If they could enter the basements of the oldest buildings on these streets, we explain, they could still see, etched on the old brick walls, the lines left by the waters of the bay.

You and your kids can develop a similar nature walk for your city by doing a little research, talking to knowledgeable people, and using your imagination.

First, do some exploring. Take your kids through the downtown area of your city with *pencil and paper* in hand. List the locations of the trees planted along the streets as well as those of any street-corner gardens or miniparks. Explore the public areas in and around major buildings. Note the color, size, and location of fire hydrants and other water sources. Write down the names of streets, parks, and plazas. Then choose a route you think would make an interesting nature walk.

Now you and your kids are ready to do some background research. Contact the following people and agencies in your city, tell them about your project, and ask them to assist you in your information search:

1. *The public works department.* Ask for the person in charge of street tree planting. Find out the species of trees planted downtown, their native countries, and the reasons they were chosen for their particular location in your city.

2. *The public relations director or building manager in each building you wish to feature.* Ask for information about the kinds and amounts of materials used in the building's construction and the geographical origins of these materials. If the building employs a gardener, ask him or her about the plants and soil used in landscaping. Why were these chosen and where do they come from?

3. *The fire department.* Ask for information on hydrants. What do the sizes and colors mean? How much water pressure does each one carry? Where does the water come from? How is pressure maintained?

4. *The geology department of your local college or university.* Request information about the soil and rock formations beneath your city. Ask about the composition and formation of building stones used in the major buildings you investigated. Find out whether a student can take you on a geology tour of the district to identify building stones and tell you how each type was formed.

5. *The city planning department.* Ask for maps and photos of your city fifty or a hundred years ago. Find out why your city was built on its particular location and whether any interesting stories can be told about how the area was developed.

6. *The public library.* If you have any questions left, research them here. Ask the librarian for old photos and maps of the city you can copy.

Now that you've collected this wealth of information, you and your kids need to develop it into good stories you can tell along the route of your nature walk. After you've tried out your guided tour on friends and family, offer it to out-of-town visitors, neighbors, scout troops, senior-citizen groups, business associations, and school groups. Once you've polished your downtown nature walk, try publishing it. Your tour and guidebook could serve as fundraisers for your organization, if you belong to one. You might even inspire local civic groups to erect plaques or sponsor exhibits based on your research.

7. city
SYSTEMS

1. HOW DOES A CITY GET ENOUGH TO EAT?

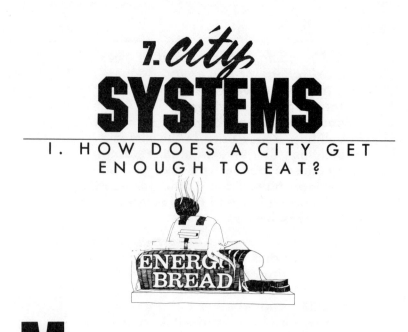

MANY PEOPLE THINK OF A CITY, especially a big one, as a cold, inanimate aggregate of concrete and steel. We're proposing quite the opposite.

A CITY IS A LIVING BEING

Think of the many ways a city resembles a living creature. Goods and natural resources flow through a city much as food does through a body. Every city, large or small, consumes millions of barrels of oil to fuel its machinery and thousands of tons of food to feed its human inhabitants. Beneath a city's streets, gas, water, and electricity course through a maze of cables and pipes that resemble a network of veins and arteries. Not unlike nervous impulses carrying data to the brain, information travels through a city's telephone lines and computer cables and is broadcast throughout the urban body through radio and television waves. In a city, birth and death occur continually as the organism develops, decays, and, perhaps after centuries, dies. One can even make a case for reproduction. Cities often give birth to suburbs, which, in turn, become cities themselves.

When we view a city as an organism, we see more clearly how its various parts and systems connect with one another. How could the food system function if the transportation system weren't healthy? The tomatoes and green beans might never make it to market, and restaurants would run out of meat and cheese. If the discard management system suddenly ground to a halt, these markets and restaurants would soon smother in their own boxes, banana peels, and beer cans. Their sinks would stop, and their toilets would no longer flush.

Besides depending on internal systems to function, a city, like an ant or an elephant, depends for survival on a network of connections with the outside world. For most cities, this ecosystem is planetary in scale. We need only ask local shopkeepers where their merchandise comes from or trace the sources of the electricity in our streetlights and the water in our sink pipes to discover that our city lives are intimately connected with cornfields in Nebraska, coffee plantations in Colombia, textile mills in India, and icy streams in the Sierra, the Rockies, or whatever mountain range is nearest.

The more we view our city or town as a whole organism, sustained by a larger whole or ecosystem, the more we can help this place we call home to live and thrive in ways that do not destroy its own support systems.

This chapter and the following one give you and your kids suggestions for exploring two systems essential to your city's health: its food and its discard management systems. You'll learn everything from how to garden in an area as small as an apartment balcony to how to turn garbage into art. Sprinkled throughout are tales of our own adventures with kids in supermarkets and at trash plants. We hope these entice you and your band of explorers to investigate similar ordinary and exotic sites in your city or town.

FEEDING A CITY

Cities are not only living organisms but hungry ones as well. Imagine the breakfasts, dinners, lunches, and snacks gobbled by a medium-sized city of one hundred thousand. If every resident eats the equivalent of 3 meals a day, in a year the city's population consumes a total of almost 110 million meals. In New York City, with its more than seven million residents, this yearly meal total reaches 8 billion. No wonder Americans spend more than $400 billion a year on food, and the food industry is the nation's largest.

Where does this food come from and what happens to it on its way to the cities? Most of the time we don't think about these questions. We simply go to the nearest supermarket and help ourselves to whatever we need or want without considering the enormous amounts of energy and organization that go into bringing our food items into such easy reach.

In this chapter we take a look at our food system and how it developed over the last 150 years, and we provide suggestions for how you and your kids can explore this strange and complex beast. We tell how, in our own work with city kids, we have explored farms, farmers' markets, community gardens, bakeries, supermarkets, and mom-and-pop grocery stores without going more than a few miles outside the city. We also describe three games that can help you and your kids view food in fresh ways. For those of you seeking the ultimate in fresh food, we explain step-by-step how you and your kids can grow your own, even if you don't have a backyard.

FROM FRESH TO FROZEN TO FOODLESS: HOW OUR FOOD SYSTEM EVOLVED

Today at any supermarket we can buy bananas from Ecuador, grapefruit from Texas, cheese from France, beef from Iowa, crabmeat from Formosa, and spices from Indonesia. But how did we city dwellers feed ourselves in the days before trucks, planes, ships, and trains converged on our major cities every day bringing boxed, canned, frozen, and bottled foods from around the globe? What did our food markets look like a century or even fifty years ago?

Until the 1930s, self-service supermarkets didn't exist, and a century ago most Americans lived on

**Between 1940 and 1978 independent
(nonchain) grocery stores declined from
446,350 to 169,500.**
—*Everybody's Business*

---------------------- * ----------------------

farms and grew a good deal of their own food. Even those
who lived in cities often had gardens in their backyards.
Some even raised milk cows, goats, and chickens there.
When they went to the store, it was usually to buy staples
in bulk or special packaged goods. The fresh stuff—milk,
eggs, vegetables, fish—was produced locally, or at least re-
gionally, and often delivered door-to-door. The large-scale,

centralized agriculture and the long-distance, high-volume food distribution and marketing we know today didn't firmly take hold until the era of so-called cheap energy after the Second World War.

Americans began fleeing the farms and flooding the cities long before that, however, and, beginning in the early nineteenth century, technologies emerged that allowed food to travel longer distances between producer and consumer without spoiling. The tin can arrived as early as 1910 and, with it, the ability to preserve cooked meat, fruit, and vegetables indefinitely. Before the turn of the century, Nabisco had taken crackers out of the barrel and put them in wax-paper-lined cartons, Borden was putting milk in individual glass bottles instead of bulk ten-gallon cans, and Chase & Sanborn was marketing roasted coffee in sealed cans, rather than selling beans by the pound in bulk. Thirty years later, by the time of the Great Depression, food processing had become big business. Kraft, the first company to process cheese, was marketing Velveeta, Birdseye was freezing green peas, and Continental Baking was perfecting Wonder Bread.

Cities like New York no longer had to rely on nearby farmers to rush fresh foods to market. The processed, packaged foods coming off the assembly lines could travel long distances by train or truck and sit in storage or on grocers' shelves for months. This meant supermarket chains could buy in bulk at discounts, and vast agricultural concerns could concentrate food production in a few choice areas of the country. This also put mom-and-pop grocery stores and family farms on the endangered species list.

Today the food industry has carried processing, packaging, efficiency, and centralization to the ultimate

---------------------------------- * ----------------------------------

How healthy are your city's veins and arteries? Find out how many work hours are spent each year repairing underground pipes and cables.

**How much water does your city drink
each day? Where does it come from?**

———————————— * ————————————

with such foodless foods as nondairy creamer and such
fast-food outlets as McDonald's. At the same time, ironically,
the rise of the natural-foods movement is leading even the
most highly centralized supermarkets to stock unprocessed,
chemical-free foods in bulk, not unlike the markets of yester-
year.

(Our main source for this information is *Everybody's Business* edited by Milton Moskowitz, Michael
Katz and Robert Levering. See bibliography.)

FOODTRIPPING WITH KIDS

With no more cows in the backyard and few family farms
nearby, city kids—and grownups—often have no idea
where their food comes from or what it looks like on vine
or hoof. City kids who have never traveled farther than the
nearest supermarket for their sustenance grow up thinking
milk comes in cartons, wheat is white, and meat is no different from textured vegetable protein. In our food field trips
with kids, we have tried to give them a better understanding
of the sources of their food, the global network of farmers
and food workers who make their meals possible, and the
options they have as consumers.

We have been fortunate in the San Francisco
Bay Area to find not only supermarkets, commercial bakeries, and burger stands but also mom-and-pop grocery
stores, Italian delicatessens, pasta factories, Chinese fish
markets, collectively run bread bakeries, food-buying clubs,
farmers' markets, community gardens, and even produce
farms. We have also found grocers, store managers, gardeners, and food plant workers willing both to talk about and
give us behind-the-scene glimpses of their food operations.
While you might not find quite this diversity if you live in a
small city, you are sure to find some options to standard
supermarket fare, even if nothing more than neighbors put-

ting up fruits and vegetables in their kitchens.

Our usual approach, one we have used with kids from six to sixteen, involves touring three different kinds of markets, usually a supermarket, a collectively run community grocery store, and a direct-sale farmers' market. Whenever possible, we have arranged interviews with the market managers and coordinated our visits with times when the stores are not too busy. To further avoid mobbing a store, we have often divided into teams and visited with only six to ten kids at a time.

Before heading out, we develop tasks for— or, when possible, with—our coexplorers. Often we draw up charts for comparison shopping that include such categories as price, quality, and service. Even six-year-old members of our food safaris have compared prices in supermarkets and small grocery stores. We have helped these and older kids develop interview questions for the managers and clerks. The interviews usually include queries about where their staples and produce come from, how these travel to the store, why they are packaged and displayed in certain ways, and what happens to them when they wilt or their shelf life expires. At the farmers' markets, kids often have a chance to talk directly with the farmers and their families about growing and selling produce.

With one energetic group of teenagers, we rose one morning well before dawn and traveled to San Francisco's wholesale produce market. Since the truckers, sellers, and greengrocers had arrived at least three hours before us, we found only a few stragglers. But we saw enough of the operation to imagine the predawn scene: scores of semis converging on the row of loading docks with their cargoes of lettuce, peaches, and asparagus from California's Central Valley; and dozens of sellers and grocers, some of whom have been rising this early five or six days a week for decades, swarming among the crates of produce and haggling over prices and quality. Even in the peaceful aftermath of this hustle and bustle, our kids sensed the excitement of the place. They chatted with the managers and truckers, inspected some remaining crates of melons

*

In 1981, according to a Gallup survey, 38 million home gardens produced the equivalent of $16 billion worth of products, slightly more than the value of all California's crops put together.

—*Newsweek,* July 25, 1982

and green beans, and returned home better appreciating the amounts of fossil fuel and human energy involved in bringing a city's food to market.

Another day we took a busload of seven-year-olds to an organic farm some twenty miles north of San Francisco on the coast. Green Gulch Farm, operated by a Zen Buddhist community, provides premium vegetables and flowers to a small produce store, a restaurant, and a cafe in the city. Watching the women and men hoe and harvest by hand, the kids learned how small farmers, relying more on people power than machinery, can grow large quantities of vegetables on very little land with minimal use of fossil fuels. They also realized, after visiting the businesses this farm supplies, what a tiny fraction of the city this farm feeds.

In a school in Berkeley, across the bay from San Francisco, we tried a hands-on approach to learning about food. First-graders and second-graders cooperated in a buying and breadbaking project. The older kids did the shopping, comparing prices and products at two different kinds of markets, and the younger ones the baking. Both shared in the fruits—or bread—of their combined labors. At one of the markets, a natural-foods store with its own bakery on the premises, the second-graders observed small-scale commercial breadbaking in operation, from the grinding of the flour to the cooling of the finished loaves on steel racks. The kids even had a chance to grind their own flour from wheat berries they had weighed out and purchased in bulk.

Back at school, these young buyers and bakers learned some energy facts about bread. With the help of a film called *Toast,* they traced the energy involved in each step of the process that brings a slice of toast to the table, from the planting of the wheat to the popping of the bread into the toaster. (See How Many Energy Steps to a Slice of Toast? on page 133 for details.)

Our visit to Clementina Garden, a community garden in the heart of industrial San Francisco, provided a sharp contrast to the supermarkets and semis of the mainstream food system. Here, through the love and hard work of the retired residents of nearby Clementina Towers,

Between 1920 and 1980 the number of farms in the United States declined from 6.5 million to 2.8 million.
—*Everybody's Business*

——————————————— * ———————————————

a former trash-filled vacant lot had been transformed into a place of beauty and nourishment. Working in the garden, using techniques passed down through generations, these old people raised spirits as well as cucumbers, cabbage, bok choy, and eggplant. In the process, they became happier, more self-reliant city dwellers. Erica best describes our visit to this magical place:

> *One day the fifth-graders at Bessie Carmichael School and their teacher walked with Carolyn and me through the industrial traffic and choking fumes of Folsom Street to a secret destination. We hurried across busy intersections and shouted to one another over unmuffled engines. After skidding along blocks of greasy, rain-soaked sidewalks and weaving between the cars lining a narrow alley, we arrived at a high cyclone fence woven with laths and a gate secured with a chain and lock. The magic of living things lay behind this dark barrier. We were about to enter Clementina Community Garden.*
>
> *Our guide unlocked the gate for us and pushed it aside. Shocked by the brilliant green light reflecting off the lush foliage, we stood motionless. Just before us lay a tiny pond lined with carefully chosen pieces of rubble. At one end a miniature windmill made of scrap tin and wood creaked in the afternoon breeze. Here and there, earth, dumped in mounds, had been molded and terraced in the Asian manner by the elderly residents of nearby Clementina Towers.*
>
> *Several of these gardeners knelt beside their plots, harvesting and weeding with*

total concentration. The children, the initial
spell broken, traveled the narrow paths
with high excitement, asking questions of
the kneeling gardeners and receiving tastes
of strange and wonderful plants. Both
children and adults sensed the love that
helped this garden grow, and something in
each of us responded mightily to life.

Clementina Community Garden no longer exists. It has
given way to additional housing for seniors. But gardening
still thrives among the residents of Clementina Towers and
their neighbors in nearby apartment complexes. The building that rose on the site of the former community garden did
not destroy green space; it raised it to new levels. Today
seniors in the Ceatrice Polite Apartments garden in raised
planting containers on the roof. Woolf House, an adjoining
senior apartment building, boasts both a rooftop garden
and a wheelchair-accessible courtyard garden. One block
away, the Alice Street Community Garden provides 300 garden spaces—plus water and the services of a landscape
consultant—free of charge to seniors in the area. Dozens of
Clementina Towers residents now tend their cabbage, bok
choy, and exotic herbs here.

 TIPS FOR TRIPS

- Find out what food-processing and
  food-packaging plants exist in your
  community. Is there a bottling plant, a
  cannery, or a commercial bakery?
  Many firms provide free tours.

- Ask your local grocers or supermarket
  managers where they obtain their produce and staples. Then find out whether
  you can visit any of the wholesale marketing and distributing operations. Perhaps your city has a wholesale produce
  market you can visit.

- Find out whether any farmers sell their produce directly to consumers in or near your city—at a farmers' market, at roadside stands, or off the back of a truck on a busy city street.

- Visit natural-foods stores. Ask the clerks or managers where they get their food. You might learn about local producers or cooperatives that would be willing to give you and your kids interviews or tours.

- Find out whether any food-buying clubs or community gardens exist in your area. Check with community service organizations, such as senior citizens' centers.

- Check with the community services department at your city hall, the local library, or the agricultural extension in your area for leads on food-related projects or businesses you can visit. Your local chamber of commerce may also be able to provide information.

- If you're exploring with a group of six or more, make appointments at the food operations you wish to visit and arrange a time that will be convenient.

FOOD GAMES

You can play these games before, during, or after your food excursions in the city. The first one, Name That Food, is a big hit anytime and works especially well in conjunction with a trip to a supermarket. We designed the second one, How Cosmopolitan Is Your Lunch?, for a lunch break on a food outing although it's also a good indoor rainy-day activity. The third, How Many Energy Steps to a Slice of Toast?,

In 1850 more than eighty percent of America's people lived on farms. Today less than four percent do.
—*Everybody's Business*

——————————————— ✱ ———————————————

can also be played any time in any number of forms but serves especially well as preparation for or follow-up to a trip to a commercial bakery or other type of food-processing plant.

Name That Food
Have you ever tried guessing the name of a food from the list of ingredients on the can or box? You might be surprised by how difficult this is, especially for some of the more processed and preserved foods on the supermarket shelves today. We found that not only do kids love to play this game, but they also learn a lot about nutrition doing so. All you need are *paper and pens* for recording.

You can start with the foods on your own kitchen shelves, but, to track down the most exotic lists of ingredients, head with your kids to the nearest supermarket. See who can find the longest list of ingredients, the one toughest to guess, or the one with the most unrecognizable words in it. As a twist, you might read the ingredients list in reverse order. The variations are endless. When you return, have a guessing game. If you're foodtripping with a group of six or more, you might play this in teams.

How Cosmopolitan Is Your Lunch?
The next time you and your kids are on a food outing and you pull out your brown bags for lunch, stop before you chomp into those sandwiches and try to figure out where they came from. Not where you bought the bread and cheese and mayonnaise, but where the wheat was grown for the flour, where the cow grazed while producing the milk for the cheese, and where the chickens roosted while laying eggs that went into the mayonnaise. You'll never know, for sure, of course, unless the bread label states, as one does,

"whole wheat flour freshly stoneground from Deaf Smith County organically grown hard red winter wheat." But you can have a lot of fun guessing, and your guessing might pique your or your kids' curiosity enough to send you to the encyclopedia or the library to find out where in the world the dill weed in your tuna salad sandwich is grown. Because the United States is the world's largest food exporter, many of the ingredients in your lunch will have domestic origins, but some, like the herbs and spices, will take you on a trip around the world.

In this game you might give prizes for "The Most All-American Lunch," "The Most Eastern-Flavored Lunch," and so on. You might also guide your kids on a global imaginary journey. Ask them to picture the foods in their lunch traveling from each item's country or state of origin to their lunch bag. Suggest that they imagine ships, trains, planes, and trucks carrying the ingredients of their sandwich to processing plants, distribution centers, and eventually local food markets.

When you're back indoors, tack *a map of the world* onto the wall and indicate on it the travels of your lunches by drawing lines or stretching lengths of *colored yarn* from the areas where your lunch food was produced to your home city. This will help you estimate the number of miles your food traveled to reach your lunch bag.

How Many Energy Steps to a Slice of Toast?
Or a frozen vegetable? Or a can of cola?

———————————————— ∗ ————————————————

A one-pound loaf of white, store-bought bread contains approximately 1250 calories, while it takes approximately 2075 calories to produce the bread and transport it to a grocery store. What is the net energy loss?

—*Energy, Food and You*

We used this game in its toast form to prepare kids for a visit to a commercial bakery. You can use it in any form to prepare kids for a visit to any kind of food-processing or food-packaging plant. It also works well as a follow-up exercise.

The point of the game is to trace the energy pathway of an item of food from the time it's produced to the time it's consumed. You can take the game a step further, if you wish, by tracing the energy steps involved in disposing of any leftovers. To keep it simple, focus only on steps requiring oil or electricity. Have *chalk and a chalkboard or markers and a large piece of butcher paper* handy so you and your kids can diagram the steps as you figure them out. You can later turn your diagram into a poster, illustrated with your own drawings or with magazine cutouts.

In tracing the energy steps, start as far back as you wish. In our toast game, we started with the fossil fuel required to prepare the wheat fields for planting: the gas to fuel the tractor and the petroleum-based fertilizer to add nutrients to the soil. We also included a tragic ending: burnt toast that had to be hauled away—by a diesel-burning truck, of course—to the dump. We usually showed the film *Toast* when we played this game. In ten minutes and with hardly more than ten words it shows the energy steps involved in producing and distributing bread. And kids love its lively musical score. (See Resources on page 183 for information on obtaining the film.) We have also found the following chart and illustration, based on the film, helpful in discussing the energy of bread production and distribution.

——————————————— * ———————————————

Since 1965, as the human birth rate declined, the pet population in the United States soared. Today pet foods occupy more supermarket space than any other food category and are more profitable as well.

—*Everybody's Business*

**4 slices to create and spread
petro-fertilizer
1 slice to raise hybrid grain
1 slice to mill grain into flour
4 slices to package flour and transport it
to bakery
1 slice to bake the bread
11 slices to process, market, and package
the bread
1 slice to transport it to the store
1 slice to transport to transport the bread
home
1 slice to truck burned toast to dump**

25 slices = no net energy profit

More energy-intensive than the commercial production and distribution of bread is that of frozen foods and canned soft drinks. Here's a list of the steps involved in producing and distributing a frozen vegetable. Figure out with your kids which steps can be eliminated. We encourage you to develop similar lists for other foods and beverages.

HOW MANY FROZEN VEGETABLE ENERGY STEPS CAN YOU REMOVE?

1. A farmer grows the vegetables.

2. Trucks or trains transport them to a processing plant.

3. Machines slice, chop, and otherwise process the vegetables.

4. Machines package them.

5. A freezer unit freezes the packages of vegetables.

6. A freezer truck or railcar transports them to a distribution center.

7. A freezer truck delivers the packages to the market.

8. The market keeps them frozen.

9. Someone in your family drives to market to buy a package and returns.

10. The freezer in your home keeps the package frozen.

11. Someone in your family cooks the vegetables.

12. They throw away the package.

13. You eat the vegetables.

(For more energy- and food-related games and for suggestions for using and expanding the above activities, see *Energy, Food, and You: An Interdisciplinary Curriculum Guide.* Information on obtaining it is listed in the bibliography under Washington State Office of Public Instruction.)

HOW TO GROW A CONTAINER GARDEN

We've known city dwellers who, with nothing but an apartment balcony for a garden, have used containers to grow fixings for soups and salads six months out of the year. All you and your kids need to do the same is *a square of yard, porch, or balcony that receives four to six hours of direct sun each day* and *a few miscellaneous containers, each at least one foot deep and wide.*

Follow these five steps:

1. *Gather containers.* Almost anything will do: wooden crates, leaky buckets, old-fashioned bushel baskets, white plastic buckets, old styrofoam coolers, plastic wastepaper baskets. You can often find large wooden crates at Chinese markets and white plastic buckets at delicatessens and restaurants.

If you use watertight containers, you might want to drill holes in the bottoms for drainage, although this is not essential. Drainage could prove a problem, especially if you are gardening on a third-floor balcony that

drains directly into the balcony of your second-floor neighbor. You might solve such problems by lining any containers that are not watertight with heavy black plastic. Add a few inches of gravel to the bottom of each container to prevent accumulated water from leading to root rot or plant disease.

One advantage watertight containers have over others is that they do not need to be watered as often. You simply must be careful not to overwater. Plastic containers have the added benefit of not rusting.

2. *Gather soil and other planting materials.* If you have a bit of soil available and you have been composting or operating a worm farm (see How-tos on pages 150 and 153), you possess all the planting material you need. If neither of the above apply, you will need to buy some planting soil from your local nursery or plant store. One seasoned container-gardener suggests filling the bottom portion of your containers with fallen deciduous leaves. If you don't have enough, your neighbors will love you for gathering theirs. The leaves will decay to humus over the course of the season and provide your plants with nutrients and beneficial microorganisms. (We found this and other ideas mentioned here in Barbara Daniels's unpublished booklet *Growing Plants in Containers: New Guidelines for a Deck Garden.*)

3. *Enrich your planting medium with plant food regularly.* You can use commercial plant food, available at supermarkets and nurseries, or you can make your own. Two books you will find helpful are John Jeavon's *How to Grow More Vegetables* and The Farallones Institute's *The Integral Urban House: Self-Reliant Living in the City* (see bibliography).

4. *Choose and plant seeds.* Although you can grow full-sized vegetables in containers, you and your kids might want to try some of the many midget varieties now available. For container gardening, you don't have to worry about planting in rows or spacing seeds as far apart as the directions say. Simply scatter them on well-soaked soil and cover to the proper depth with an added layer of soil. You can thin later. Try growing two or more kinds of vegetables together—tomatoes and carrots, for instance. Tomatoes, broccoli, cucumbers, and squash appreciate two feet of soil, but lettuce, radishes, and stubby carrots can thrive in as little as six inches.

5. *Water your container plants.* Do so from the top only, using a gentle stream or spray. Wait until the soil has dried out to a depth of an inch or so before watering again. To gauge the depth of soil moisture, insert wooden sticks—popsicle sticks and wooden chopsticks work well—into each container. If you don't have a hose handy for watering, try recycling water from your shower or bathtub. Keep a plastic bucket in the shower stall or tub to catch the water that would otherwise go down the drain while you are waiting for the stream to warm up.

8. city SYSTEMS

II. TAKING CARE OF LEFTOVERS

OST OF US CITY DWELLERS carry out the garbage at least once a week and take for granted it will be hauled away, just as we assume our toilets will flush and our showers will drain. Unless we are avid recyclers, the only time we and our kids come face to face with the discards our city generates is when we take a trip to the local dump after our annual pruning of trees or cleaning of the basement. Then we usually pay our fee, drive home, and forget about the mess for another year.

Ours isn't the only society that has taken an out-of-sight, out-of-mind attitude toward discarded materials. Even our Native American predecessors on the land piled their garbage outside their villages and forgot about it. For them this didn't pose a problem. They generated only a fraction of the waste we accumulate today, and theirs was organic and harmless to the biosphere.

Near San Francisco Bay, a mound three hundred feet in diameter and ten feet high contains everything the Ohlone Indians of the area ate, wore, used, and lived in for almost four thousand years. In contrast, the dump trucks of the nine Bay Area counties today haul enough solid waste to fill the Oakland Coliseum to the brim every day.

Despite the fact that urban solid wastes doubled between 1960 and 1980, cities continue to dispose of ninety percent of their garbage on land. Before the end of the decade, nearly half of all major cities will exhaust their landfill capacity. In other words, if we city dwellers don't change our ways of handling garbage in a hurry, we'll soon be buried by it. Some people believe the only solutions are costly ones: hauling it farther, burning it in expensive plants, or separating it for recycling with complicated mechanical devices. Others claim that labor-intensive recycling efforts will solve the problem without bankrupting the taxpayers or stressing the ecosystem. No matter which path our cities take, our kids are sure to inherit a world in which the disposing of discards is a major issue.

Our choice of words in discussing this issue may contribute to the problem in subtle ways. Using the word *waste* to refer to everything we throw out means we assume that these materials have no productive value. If, instead, we call these items discards, we leave open the possibility of reusing or otherwise recycling them. Everything we throw out need not be wasted. A high percentage of it—some say as much as seventy to ninety percent of household discards—can be recycled.

Our empty glass bottles can be crushed and processed into new bottles. Other items such as newspaper, office paper, cardboard, motor oil, tin, and aluminum can also be reprocessed into usable materials. We can use our grass clippings and our kitchen scraps to make compost.

——————————————— * ———————————————

By 1990, New Jersey plans to recycle 25 percent of its household discards.
—Institute for Local Self-Reliance

Whatever scraps we don't need will be happily consumed by the nation's hogs. At this point a million hogs across the country survive on cooked, bacteria-free kitchen scraps, and millions more would love to join the feast. Even the sludge our city's sewage treatment plant produces can be turned into a nonharmful soil amendment for the lawns in our municipal parks. An increasing number of cities are recycling their sludge in this manner.

Many household discards are reusable without being processed: clothing, shoes, kitchen utensils, appliances, furniture. About the only household throwaways that can't be recycled are those containing plastic or more than one kind of metal.

TRASH TRIPS, OR FACE TO FACE WITH THE GARBAGE MONSTER

You might think exploring the trash and sewage systems in your city will seem dull or repulsive to kids. Not so. In our years of taking city kids on urban explorations, we found they always loved mucking around in garbage dumps and going underground to view sewage treatment systems.

At the Garbage Palace, as San Francisco's solid-waste transfer station is affectionately known, kids stared slack-jawed and wide-eyed as the packer trucks dumped loads of garbage into a vast, concrete pit, creating mountains of human refuse in minutes. They were amazed at the contents of the trash heaps: tables, chairs, and machinery tumbled in along with vegetable peels and cardboard cartons. All responded with oohs and aahs when Leo, our scavenger company guide, told of having found an intact piano in the pit. On one of our trips, a young boy, with the help of Leo, recovered a perfectly good basketball from the heap and happily clutched it all the way home. He and his classmates learned that one person's trash can be another's treasure.,

On our trips, we occasionally ventured underground with kids to San Francisco's sewage treatment plant and visited other places in the city not usually associated with wastes or recycling. We discovered that

Golden Gate Park processes and reuses organic debris. It enriches its compost operation with manure and straw from the riding stables and uses chips made from twigs and brush as top dressing and mulch.

———————————————— ✷ ————————————————

"California produces 46 million tons of garbage annually, enough to blanket Interstate 5 from Mexico to the Oregon border ten feet deep."
—Michelle Bekey, *California Business*, July 1982

To arrange group trash trips for your kids, call the city or county offices responsible for sewage treatment, waste management, and recycling or reclaiming operations. Find out whether your local parks department takes advantage of composting or reclaiming projects. If household garbage collection is handled by a private company, contact its offices for an interview or a tour. Often the larger sewage and garbage treatment plants offer free educational tours, slide shows, and handouts.

Even if you and your kids live in a small town without its own treatment plants, you can find plenty of ways to investigate how people in your area are disposing of or reclaiming discards. Auto wrecking yards, flea markets, second-hand and antique stores, and garage sales are all recycling operations. If you ask oldtimers how they reused things in times past, you'll probably find they were recyclers, even though they may never have described themselves that way. Before World War II and the advent of plastics and disposables, everyone was a recycler. As a project, you and your kids could compile an oral history of household recycling by interviewing grandparents and other older people you know.

Before you and your kids set out to explore your city's discard management systems, take the following quiz. If you have trouble answering most of the questions, you are probably no different from your neighbors. Few of us know what happens to our throwaways after they leave the house.

To help your kids find answers to these questions, contact the city, county, and regional offices near you that handle street cleaning, sewage treatment, garbage collection, recycling, and other such services. Local environmental and citizens' action groups may also be useful sources. Try finding more than one information source for

---

*

How might the waste of cities support further life as do the wastes of plants and animals?

each question. Do they agree? If not, why might this be? Use the quiz as an opportunity to teach your kids research skills.

LEFTOVERS QUIZ

1. Where do the garbage collection trucks take your household discards? How are these treated? How close is the system to capacity?

2. Where does the litter on your streets come from? Who is responsible for cleaning it up? Where does it go?

3. Where does the water go when you take a shower? Flush the toilet? Wash the dishes? What happens to the water that flows down the storm drain when you wash your car or water your lawn?

4. How is your sewage treated? What happens to the treated sewage? How close is the system to capacity?

5. What toxic wastes flow into the waste stream of your city? Where do they come from? Who monitors them? How are they treated? Where do they go?

6. How serious is air pollution in your city? Where does it come from? Who monitors it? Is the air quality improving or getting worse?

GARBAGE GAMES AND OTHER WASTE AND REUSE ACTIVITIES

Garbage is much maligned as a rotten, smelly urban problem threatening to gobble our land, injure our health, and deface our environment. While garbage and other throwaways can be all these things, they can also be fun and even beautiful, as the following games and activities demonstrate.

Food Waste Weigh-In

How close can you come to creating a wasteless meal? This game gives you and your kids a chance to find out. All you need is *a small scale*. To play, you weigh a meal's ingredients and packaging before preparing the meal, weigh the packaging and food scraps you have left over after the meal, and calculate the difference. To avoid arguments and cries of "Foul!" define what you mean by waste first and make some rules. For instance, do you consider the food scraps you compost waste? How about the containers you use as kindling or take to a recycling center? And what if you use only part of a can of olives? How do you calculate the waste? Make sure everyone agrees on the rules before they play the game.

After you and your kids have developed the near wasteless meal, try creating the most wasteful meal you can think of. Even if you never make this meal, planning it can be a lot of fun.

In both this game and the next, you may compete with each other as individuals or cooperate as a group, competing against your own best efforts.

Down the Drain: A Water Use Game

The point of this game is to find out how much water you and your kids use in a typical day and to devise ways to cut this quantity. Your kids may take this as a signal to revert to an unwashed state. Make sure they know that, while cutting back on water used in showering and toothbrushing is fine, cutting out the activities themselves constitutes cheating.

To play, you'll need *a bucket* and *a clock or watch*. You can estimate the amount of water you use while showering by timing how long a typical flow of water from

─────────────── ✳ ───────────────

As of 1986, New Jersey has only 11 landfill sites available. Ten years ago it had 300.

—Institute for Local Self-Reliance

the shower head takes to fill a measured bucket. Then, time your shower and estimate how many bucketsful of water you used. To estimate toilet water use, measure or estimate the water in the tank and count the number of flushes per day. If you wish to gauge the exact amount of tank water, first close the water inlet valve beneath the tank, then scoop the tank water into a measured bucket. After measuring, pour the water back into the tank. For washing machines and dishwashers, you can probably find out how much water is used for each load by checking the product literature or calling a local appliance store or the manufacturer.

For other uses, such as toothbrushing and face washing, simply catch the water in measured containers and add up the total quantities. For car-washing calculations, measure how much water flows out of the hose each quarter minute, or fifteen seconds, and multiply this by four times the number of minutes you run the hose during a typical washing.

Pollution Test: How Clean Is Your Air?

You and your kids can check the air in your neighborhood for visible pollutants such as fly ash and dust with a simple test. Lay *a sheet of white blotter paper* on a flat outdoor surface. If you can't easily obtain blotter paper, substitute any kind of white paper that will catch and hold dust and ash. Place upon the paper, in rows, *twenty-one play blocks.* Each day remove one of the blocks. By the time you remove the final block, you will have a display of visible air pollution over a three-week period.

To make an even more striking test of a source of air pollution, place *a white paper tissue or towel* over the *tail pipe of a car* while the engine is idling. Check it after ten seconds. Be sure the tailpipe is cool enough to touch before you try this test.

Indoor Garbage Gardens

The next time you're preparing vegetables in the kitchen, stop before you throw out that carrot top or wrinkled sweet

Scores of U.S. cities, from Los Angeles, California, to Bangor, Maine, are reclaiming, through composting, the sewage sludge they used to dump into the ocean.
—*BioCycle*

——————————————— ✳ ———————————————

potato. You and your kids can grow a garden from these leftovers. Besides growing long, lovely vines and other kinds of leafy foliage from root vegetables, you can sprout orange and apple tree seedlings and squash and melon vines from the seeds you rescue from the garbage can.

With *root vegetables,* you simply need to save a one- or two-inch portion of each root, including the stem or eye section, and place this in *a shallow bowl of water. Seeds* sprout best if you soak them overnight, then plant them in *an egg carton—or other shallow container— filled with moist potting soil.* You can transplant them to their own *pots* after they've grown an inch or two. Some seeds—such as those from peaches, plums, and apples— sprout best after wintering in your refrigerator for a month or two. From *an avocado seed* you can grow a lush, broad-leafed house plant to rival that in any plant shop. Simply wash the seed, stick *three toothpicks,* equidistant from one another, around its middle, and balance the seed, pointed end up, in *a glass of water.*

For more details on growing gardens from garbage, see Linda Allison's *The Reasons for Seasons* (in bibliography).

If you're serious about gardening, outdoors as well as in, consider saving your kitchen scraps and turning them into compost or letting worms do the work for you. For instructions on how to make your own compost and how to start a worm farm in very little space, see pages 150 and 153, respectively.

Trash Art
A number of artists, including California sculptor Art Grant and New York experimental artist Sari Dienes, have become

highbrow recyclers, raising trash of all kinds to the level of an art form.

You and your kids can join the ranks of these trash artists by bringing a garbage bag along on your next city expedition and picking up waste materials for sculptures and collages as you explore. Public dumps or landfill sites are rich in raw materials for such artworks. Why not combine a trash art project with your next visit to the dump?

TRASH ART PROJECT IDEAS

● *Monumental nothings.* Create, in teams, giant junk sculptures with no obvious useful functions.

● *Junk music.* Form a band that plays instruments made solely out of throwaways and hold junk jam sessions.

● *Trash town.* Design a model town that embodies every kid's fantasies using discarded materials only.

● *Rummaged rumpus.* Convert an old shed or an unused corner of a room or garage into a playroom using only rummaged materials.

*

Some birds are veritable junk collectors. One Redtail hawk used, in the base of its nest, two kilograms of odds and ends, including 361 stones, 15 nails, 146 pieces of board, 14 bamboo splinters, three pieces of tin, 35 old pieces of adhesive tape, 103 pieces of hard dirt, 30 pieces of horse manure, several pieces of rags and bones, one piece of glass, and four pieces of old inner tube.
—Joel Carl Welty, *The Life of Birds*

HOW TO COMPOST IN A CAN

One way to reduce our household wastes and get rich for our efforts is by composting. Food scraps can be easily turned into garden gold—dark, moist, nutrient-rich compost—by a process that takes up no more space than a garbage can. With the following method, you can actually use a garbage can as the compost bin. Instead of tossing your kitchen scraps out in a garbage can, why not try composting them in one? What better way to introduce your city-bred kids to the cycles of nature?

If done properly, backporch composting in a can produces finished compost in three to four months without creating unpleasant odors or fly problems. Your neighbors will have nothing to complain about, and you will have a complete plant fertilizer, soil amendment, and mulch, all in one.

Here's all you need to do:

1. Punch holes in the bottom of *a twenty- or thirty-gallon garbage can* and place it on *bricks or concrete blocks.* If you wish to catch the nutrient-rich drippings, place a metal pan under the bricks.

2. Gather *materials to absorb the moisture* in the compost and prevent odors and flies. Sawdust works beautifully and often can be obtained free from woodworking shops. Soil, ashes, and dry leaves also work well. These dry materials provide carbon for the compost.

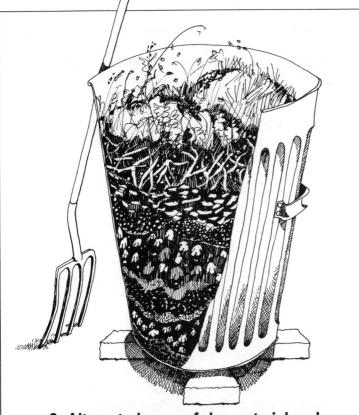

3. Alternate layers of dry material and *kitchen scraps,* making sure the scraps are always well covered. Use any food scraps except those from such fatty foods as meats and cheeses. These do not break down well and can attract animals. To speed the composting process, cut or tear large scraps into small pieces. Egg shells break down faster after they have been dried in the sun or by the pilot light of a gas oven.

4. Enrich your compost with *fresh greens or grass clippings.* These provide the nitrogen necessary to feed

the bacteria that are busily decomposing your scraps. If your kitchen scraps contain plenty of fresh greens, you may not need to enrich your mixture, but grass clippings and other fresh green garden trimmings always help. Green weeds work well so long as their roots and seeds aren't included. If you don't have garden greenery of your own, you can usually obtain clippings from a neighbor or a local gardener.

5. Occasionally enrich your mixture with *manure or other substances rich in nitrogen*. Fresh chicken, rabbit, steer, and horse manure all work well. You can often obtain manure from a local stable. If you don't mind the expense, you can add bone meal or hoof or horn meal to provide nitrogen. If your compost begins to smell of ammonia, you have added too much nitrogen. In this case, add more dried materials to correct the nitrogen-carbon ratio.

6. Aerate the compost in your can occasionally by poking *a broom or mop handle* into the mixture.

7. Once your can is full, let it sit for three or four months before using it in your garden. Ideally, you will use two cans for composting. While one is being filled, the other will be maturing.

Sources for further information on composting include John Jeavon's *How to Grow More Vegetables* and The Farallones Institute's *The Integral Urban House: Self-Reliant Living in the City* (see bibliography).

HOW TO MAKE A WORM FARM IN A BOX

If you and your kids love the idea of composting but don't have the patience to wait three or four months for the process to finish, you can cut the time in half by composting with the help of a few worm friends. Earthworms love to burrow through kitchen scraps, and their castings, which resemble coffee

grounds, are five times richer than most fertile soil and loaded with microorganisms. What's more, these humble creatures will happily work their miracles in a modest wooden box —or garbage can—on the back porch. All you need do is keep feeding the critters.

Here's how you and your kids can start your own worm farm and soil factory:

1. Find or make a container. *A twenty- or thirty-gallon garbage can or a wooden crate of comparable size* will do. Since worms prefer moist, dark places, cover the box or can with *a loose-fitting lid.*

2. Obtain some earthworms. Ordinary garden worms won't do. You need the *red wrigglers* that bait and tackle shops carry. These are the most prolific eaters and breeders and are best able to withstand changes in temperature.

3. Gather *soil.* If you don't have soil in your yard or around the edges of your house or apartment building, find someone who does or buy some of the sterilized variety at a nursery or plant shop. Worms prefer soil that is damp but not muddy.

4. Plant a handful of worms—at least four—in a two-to-three-inch layer of soil in your container. Cover with a layer of *fruit and vegetable scraps* and another layer of soil. Continue adding scraps and soil each day. Once you have a good base of soil you need not layer each time. Simply stir in the

scraps well. Earthworms prefer scraps that are small in size and not too acidic. Avoid tomatoes and citrus fruit. Other than this, the wrigglers will eat most anything, including coffee grounds, vacuum cleaner dust, and shredded newspaper and cardboard. These *dry materials* will absorb the excess moisture from your kitchen scraps and keep your mixture from getting soggy.

5. Aerate the mixture several times a week by punching deep holes in it with *a broom or mop handle.*

6. Enrich the mixture occasionally with *grass clippings, compost, or manure.* (Worms like treats, too.)

7. When the can or box is full, let the mixture sit for one and a half to two months before using it in your garden.

8. Transfer a portion of the worm-rich compost to *a second container* and start anew. Or, harvest the earthworms by spreading the compost on *a tarp* in the sun. Reacting to the heat, light, and dryness, the worms will cluster in sticky balls and can be easily picked up and transferred to a new home.

*

Plants "wash" the air. They transpire large quantities of water into the atmosphere, which helps to settle out windborne pollutants.

—*Gardens for All News*

9. *taking* ACTION

E'VE DESIGNED THE TREASURE HUNTS, ecology games, mime activities, and interviews of this book to help you and your kids explore the city with fresh vision. They help you spy on the secret lives of its bugs and flowers; investigate the blooming, buzzing yet ordered confusion of its parks and vacant lots; and grasp the astounding complexity of its network of human support systems.

So what do you do with this vision of life in your city? Perhaps you need not do anything except continue to view your city whole and appreciate its myriad forms of life. Maybe the best thing you can do is enjoy your neighborhood and its many inhabitants, treating all with respect and thoughtfulness.

If, however, you and your kids feel the urge to do something more, you can start just about anywhere. You can plant a garden, organize a neighborhood street fair, or start a recycling center. In developing these projects, you adults need not automatically take the lead. Kids, we have learned, can be just as interested in and capable of carrying out neighborhood or city action projects as adults.

In our own work with kids and in our research for this book, we have discovered that thousands of city kids today are not waiting until they are old enough to vote to begin purposefully shaping their environments. In the Bronx, New York, seventy junior high school students organized to pressure city officials to tear down several abandoned buildings. In their place, the kids developed a garden for themselves and their schoolmates. In Dublin, California, a Girl Scout troop planted hundreds of evergreen trees on a hillside behind a senior citizens' center. And in Wallingford, Connecticut, a half dozen high school students, on their own initiative, conducted energy audits and recommended conservation measures that saved their school district $350,000.

We're sure that for all the hundreds of kids we've worked with or heard about who are taking positive action to improve their cities, thousands more are carrying out projects in their homes, schools, and neighborhoods without publicity. We've found that, when given a chance, even the most streetwise kids are eager to channel their energies constructively into community projects, provided they can have a say in these and are supported but not dominated by adults in their efforts.

Our adult attitudes present some of the biggest stumbling blocks to kid-planned projects. For centuries we've been conditioned to think that kids don't know what they want and that even if they did, they wouldn't know how to go about getting it. Another obstacle is our ignorance about how kids most effectively plan and organize activities. The mode best for kids may not look at all like the way adults plan and organize. Ten- and twelve-year-olds are not likely to be comfortable with the formality of committees, parliamentary procedures, and boardrooms. If we adults want to support kids in organizing their own projects or include them in the planning process for our projects, we may have to drop some of our traditional planning models and experiment with approaches better suited to kids.

Urban planning projects and research experiments in other countries have shown that even kids as young as seven years not only know what they want but can communicate this when allowed to express themselves in ways with which they feel comfortable.

In Oslo, Norway, planners developing one of the older sections of the city gathered the views of seven- to twelve-year-olds about how they would like to see their neighborhood change. The planners found that the younger kids expressed themselves best by drawing pictures, the older kids by writing stories.

In Rotterdam, the Netherlands, a group of eleven- to fourteen-year-olds participated even more fully in an urban renewal project. They conducted research, drafted a proposal—complete with drawings, photos, traffic reports, and other data—and presented their findings and recommendations to the city aldermen at a public meeting. To develop their plan of action, these kids used role playing, taking the parts of city officials, residents, police, journalists, and children. (For more information on these and other examples of city planning with children in mind, see Westland and Knight's *Playing, Living, Learning,* listed in bibliography.)

In both these examples kids helped plan by playing; they drew pictures, told stories, and role-played parts. We grownups might not only support them in this process but learn from them as well. With fewer committee meetings and more storytelling sessions, we might plan more playful, attractive cities.

We also have a great deal to offer kids. They look to us for much of the skill, experience, and information necessary to carry out their projects. Our challenge is to offer this to them without dominating the decision-making process. The more we can do this, the better our kids can learn not only how to build planters, organize community gardens, and run recycling programs, but also how to function responsibly and creatively in a democracy.

*

Every summer in Milwaukee, Wisconsin, inner-city children turn out to tend garden plots provided by the *Shoots 'n Roots Program.* Some help disabled elderly people plant and tend their plots.

In helping kids plan and implement community projects, we learned the importance of the following three practical steps:

1. Set specific, attainable goals. Define these clearly at the beginning, making sure every member of the group, including the youngest, has helped develop these and understands them and the steps toward them.

2. Be sure the people affected by the project have a chance to participate, even if only to express their opinions. If you're planting street trees, for instance, let the people living nearby know what you're doing and why, even if you have no legal obligation to do so. You may turn potential critics into enthusiastic boosters.

3. If your project requires agreements with neighbors, city officials, or others outside your group, be sure to obtain permissions and promises in writing to prevent disappointment and confusion later.

*

In one big-city neighborhood where recreation facilities were chronically vandalized, an architect involved the local children in the designing and building of a new playground. Throughout the project not one incident of theft or willful damage occurred.

—*Childhood City Newsletter*

The tools this book offers you for exploring the city can also be used in helping kids take action. Treasure hunts, imaginary journeys, role playing, interviewing, make-believe television shows, and miming and moving are all ways you and your kids can not only find out what you and others like and don't like about your city, they can also help you devise creative plans for doing something about this.

The more young people feel they have a say in the way their neighborhoods and cities develop, the more they will take pride in improving them, and the better chance they will have—along with the rest of us—to enjoy cities that are healthy for children and all living beings.

APPENDIX:

PLANNING AND GUIDING
YOUR URBAN SAFARIS

AS A GROWNUP EXPLORING THE CITY with kids, you'll find yourself acting both as guide and explorer. If you are one of two brave adults heading downtown with twenty-five rambunctious ten-year-olds, you'll wear your guide hat much more than if you are strolling around your immediate neighborhood with your own two well-behaved children. The amount of planning and structure that goes into your urban safaris will vary with the size and age of your group.

We recommend that you keep your explorer's cap handy and your kid-self close to the surface no matter how carefully guided your expedition must be. Be ready for surprises, and flexible and creative enough to take advantage of them. Remember that the most fun parts of an outing can also be the most educational, even if they aren't on the agenda. When the kids spot a caterpillar, don't worry about maintaining your adult dignity. Get down on your knees to examine the creature with them—and, if necessary, to protect it from their overeager squeezes. When you pass a busy construction site, gawk along with the kids at the maneuvers of the crane operator, even though doing so throws your schedule off five minutes. Spontaneous incidents such as these can teach kids valuable lessons in how an urban ecosystem works, for plants and animals as well as people.

GUIDING CHILD ENERGY

Not all the surprises of your safari will be pleasant ones. Some may trigger your own fears as well as those of your kids. Whether pleasant or unpleasant, any surprise will require quick thinking and acting on your part. As adults who live or work with kids, you have undoubtedly developed your own strategies for responding to the unexpected, handling emotional outbursts, keeping your charges' attention, and helping them learn under wildly varying conditions. The incident we recount below is one of many that led us to develop our five keys to helping kids have a rewarding experience outdoors.

Along Came a Spider

Erica, a spider lover now, remembers a time when she wasn't so comfortable with these eight-legged creatures. One day during a picnic she had to confront her fear in the midst of a group of equally fearful young daycampers:

> *About six kids and I were sitting at a picnic table in a city park when a large brown spider came strolling across the table top. Oblivious to the chorus of shrieks and one kid's threat of instant death beneath his shoe, the spider serenely continued its journey toward the far end of the table.*

"A tear came to Wilbur's eye. 'Oh, Charlotte,' he said, 'To think that when I first met you I thought you were cruel and bloodthirsty!' "

—E. B. White, *Charlotte's Web*

———————————————— * ————————————————

I realized that, if I was going to help these kids overcome their fears and develop a sense of love and caring for all life, I would have to confront my own deep-seated fear of spiders. And I would have to act quickly. I admitted to the kids that I'd always been afraid of spiders, too, but now was the time for me to change. With creeping skin, I put my hand in the spider's path and allowed it to climb my finger. That done, the children and I began to relax. Soon our natural curiosity took over, and we found ourselves observing and learning from this most ancient of creatures. Within minutes our enemy had become a friend and teacher.

FIVE KEYS TO EXPLORING OUTDOORS WITH KIDS

1. *Focus the kids' attention.* **In the spider incident, when Erica picked up the creature the kids thought was scary, she fired their curiosity. What will happen next? they wondered. Before they knew it, they were involved and eager to learn.**

2. *Be honest about your feelings without dramatizing them.* **Kids can sense when you are scared, angry, or hurt, so it's no use pretending otherwise. But admitting your feelings is not the same as acting them out.**

When Erica spied the spider, she remained calm while admitting that she was afraid. This helped the kids in her group acknowledge their fear as well. Once a monster, like fear, is confronted and named, it tends to shrink in size. When you notice that an incident is stirring up strong feelings, give the group time and encouragement to speak about these. Join the discussion yourself. By observing how you deal with your emotions, children will learn how to handle their own.

3. *Be sensitive to the kids' moods and needs.* Your being attentive to the kids' feelings and needs can encourage them to be supportive of each other and sensitive to the larger environment. In the spider incident, Erica did not scold the children for their fearful shrieks and threats; rather, she showed understanding and concern for their feelings and showed them one way to move beyond these. Once the kids' fear had turned to wonder, they began feeling a connection with the spider, comparing, for example, its needs for food, shelter, and protection with their own. They soon became protective of the creature, viewing it as a vulnerable and valuable resident of the world.

4. *Take time for quiet observation.* Sometimes the city and its creatures reveal their secrets best when approached in silence and with focused attention. Drawing demands this sort of attention and is a fine activity to intersperse with more active group games and tasks. Asking kids to sketch a scary spider or insect you have captured temporarily in a glass jar will

not only calm them down but will also help them learn about the creature and, perhaps, begin to lose their fear of it.

5. *Use mime and imagination.* Don't just talk with your kids about their discoveries; encourage them to act these out. The kids will learn much more this way. Information will get into their bones and muscles and hearts as well as their heads. Dramatizing exciting discoveries also releases pent-up energy in constructive ways. After Erica's group observed the spider closely, they tried moving around like it, imagining how this creature must feel crawling about through a world of giants. In doing so, they learned to empathize with their newfound friend more than they could have if they had just observed and researched it. Incidents such as the spider encounter provide fertile soil for imagination and movement games, drawing, and storytelling. Don't be afraid to use these dramatic, playful learning tools.

TAKE ONLY PICTURES, LEAVE ONLY FOOTPRINTS

When Erica met the spider on the picnic table, she not only had to decide how to quickly attract the attention of the kids she was guiding but also how to teach them appropriate ways of treating wild things. In this case, the wild thing was a spider frightening the kids and their grownup guide. In other situations, the creature might be a wildflower or a squirrel or a caterpillar delighting a group of city explorers. In our delight we often yearn to prolong our contact with the natural world by returning home with a handful of flowers or a beetle we caught in a jar.

Though we do so with the best intentions, our taking even a small thing from its habitat can disrupt the

interdependencies plants and animals must maintain to survive. Flowers, for instance, contain the reproductive parts of
the plant on which they grow. A single flower may be able
to produce hundreds of seeds. Picking that flower destroys
potential seeds, reducing important sources of food for animals, and lessening the possibility of more plants establish-
ing themselves in that environment. Sometimes we do need
to gather flowers for display or dissection, but, in these
cases, one or two will do rather than a handful.

       Removing an animal, even a tiny insect, from
its habitat and not replacing it where we found it can also
affect the natural balance. The insect will no longer fulfill its

role in the food chain and might perish from exposure and lack of food.

Large rocks, pieces of broken cement, even old cardboard boxes conceal a surprising variety of wildlife. When we turn these over, we leave the protected hiding places beneath them exposed to drying sun and wind, the sharp eyes of predators, and the crunch of a misplaced step. So we need to be careful, after peeking beneath these animal homes, to return them exactly as we found them, without squashing anything as we do.

Even the most thoughtful, well-behaved explorers need reminders about these conservation practices before heading off on their expeditions. Carolyn recalls learning this lesson from an enthusiastic but uninformed group of Girl Scouts she led on one of her early urban nature walks:

> *As we left a lush hillside vacant lot to return to the meeting room, two of the scouts caught up with me, breathless and smiling. From behind their backs each brought forth a lovely bouquet of wildflowers picked just for me. I turned around to discover, to my delight and dismay, that every one of the girls had picked a similar bouquet. They looked so pleased with themselves I hardly had the heart to tell them—as I should have before the walk—the rule about not collecting living things.*

"Take only pictures, leave only footprints"—an adage familiar to wilderness hikers—might guide city explorers as well.

PLANNING MAKES PERFECT

When you're traveling in a group, whether to a neighborhood park or to city hall, planning can mean the difference between fun and frustration. We've found it helps to involve kids as much as possible. Not only can group planning sessions generate excitement and a sense of common purpose, they can also reduce considerably the time you need to spend peacekeeping on the trip. As much as kids love surprises, they also like to know what they are getting into and how they will be expected to act. In your sessions you might ask kids how they think they should behave in given situations. Have them help write the rules of conduct.

FOUR TIPS ON PLANNING AND PREPARATION

1. As a group, make a list of the kinds of experiences you most want included and discuss how you might incorporate these into your trip.

2. If you're planning a major trip with a group, bring in pictures, games, films, or speakers to provide background information and stimulate interest.

3. Pace yourselves. Balance quiet activities with active games, and be careful not to overschedule. After an hour or so of focused investigations, your brains will need time off to process the data. Plan breaks for food, rest, and unstructured play. Include restroom breaks as well, and check on the availability of facilities.

4. Ask questions that will help kids prepare themselves for the adventure. Who might we see? Who might see us? How might we feel about our surroundings? How can we best treat one another and the environment? What might be scary or challenging and how might we respond?

When to Use—and Not Use—Worksheets

While structuring activities for kids can help them focus and learn, too much structure can restrict their creativity and give them the sense that they are doing something for the adults.

If you're exploring with just two or three kids, you can easily improvise. You can poke into side alleys, follow butterflies, or chat with oldtimers as the spirit moves you. With groups of six or more, you need a structure or plan to keep the your coexplorers from going off in six different directions. We found worksheets worked well for large groups of kids who can read and write. Throughout the book you will find sample worksheets. From these you can create your own, tailored to the skill and comprehension levels of the children with whom you are exploring.

Be careful not to overuse worksheets and other written exercises. Expecting kids to translate their observations immediately into words can dull the excitement and spontaneity of the learning. It can also bias the activity in favor of the verbal learners. If you use worksheets, consider putting these aside frequently while you're exploring and observing. Let the writing be a follow-up to the experience, not a substitute for it. Allow yourselves to absorb, with undivided attention, the gifts of the city: the shiny batch of insect eggs clinging to a leaf, the miniature garden tucked between the buildings of concrete and steel, or that old person on the park bench willing to talk about the changes she or he has seen in the neighborhood. Between each adventure, with the help of worksheets, you can analyze and describe your experiences.

When you have returned, lead your kids in follow-up activities that will help them integrate and make sense of what they have learned while exploring. These might range from an informal, fifteen-minute discussion to a long-term research or action project. For starters you might ask a few questions: What was most fun? What least pleasant or interesting? What were the most important things you learned? The most surprising? What would you like to learn more about? How might we do this?

Based on your adventures you might write a play, tell a story, or make charts, graphs, or maps. You might even take action. Young explorers we know have planned trips for their friends, organized neighborhood litter pickup days, and started simple recycling projects in their homes.

Packing for the Trip

Professional wilderness explorers take great care gathering appropriate apparel and supplies before setting off on an expedition. You city explorers need not be exceptions. Before heading out the door, be sure you and your kids are dressed adequately. Check the weather to find out whether you need to bring extra sweaters, sun hats, raincoats, or galoshes, and make sure everyone is wearing comfortable walking shoes. If you're exploring with a large group, you might send a note home with each member ahead of time listing the clothing and supplies she or he will need for the trip.

While daypacks are not essential, you will find them useful on trips both short and long. Kids can stuff their notebooks and pencils, lunch bags, sweaters, and hats in these. They won't have to worry about losing their possessions or be tempted to burden their grownup guides with their paraphernalia. On page 174 you will find simple instructions for making your own daypack.

If you plan to study plants and insects, you might bring along a hand lens or a magnifying glass and a few small collecting jars. A one-meter length of string can help you stake a claim in a park or vacant lot. Binoculars can assist your birdwatching but are not essential.

You might take along a couple of sturdy plastic bags for trash collecting. You can use these to pack back your own trash, if you need to, and to leave a park or street

---

*

Which animals are you more likely to find on rainy days than on sunny ones?

cleaner than you found it. If you plan to do serious trash collecting, bring along some gloves to protect your hands.

What If It Rains?

Humans, especially grownup humans, make a big deal of rain. Rainstorms can be nasty. They can lead to wet feet, sniffly noses, flooded streets, and worse. But they can also bring out marvelous creepy, crawly things in a city's wild places. You don't have to cancel a trip outdoors at the first drop. If the rain stays a gentle drizzle and the weather remains warm, consider donning raingear and heading outdoors to find out what the other animals are up to.

Kids often love the rain and don't mind being caught in it. One of our most vivid memories is of a group of fourth-graders squealing with delight as a sudden downpour drenched them while we were exploring one of San Francisco's most wild and beautiful areas. Glen Canyon Park —a favorite of kids, rock-climbers, and naturalists—is blessed with a willow-lined creek, rough rock walls, and a multitude of salamanders, kestrels, and other wild creatures. That day we and our coexplorers were so engrossed in examining the wild radish clumps near the trail and the lichens growing on the rock outcroppings, we neglected to notice the black clouds building overhead. When the clouds finally burst, we scurried for a nearby stand of eucalyptus trees. Then we made a break for it and raced back to school like a covey of quail. After we had dried off as much as possible, we engaged in a lively discussion—and dramatization—of what animals do when it rains.

Some days, when rain comes down in buckets or snow and ice abound, you must stay indoors. But you and your child friends need not stop exploring, playing, and learning. You still have your imagination, and with it you can easily make up fun activities for yourselves. You'll find ideas for imaginary journeys, board games, and other indoor activities throughout this book.

————————————— ✷ —————————————

What is a habitat?

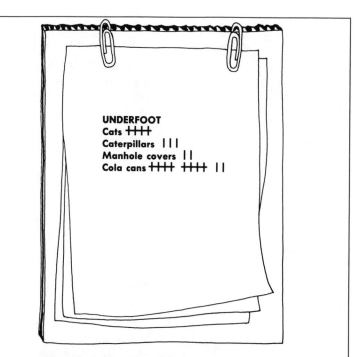

UNDERFOOT
Cats ++++
Caterpillars │││
Manhole covers ││
Cola cans ++++ ++++ ││

HOW TO MAKE A CLIPBOARD

Clipboards are especially useful when you plan to fill in worksheets, conduct interviews, take notes, or sketch plants or animals during your trips outdoors. They are easy to make. All you need are *corrugated cardboard, paperclips,* and *a knife or a pair of scissors.*

1. Cut a 10 × 12 in rectangle from a corrugated cardboard box. Be sure the corrugated lines run lengthwise.

2. Stick two sturdy paperclips into the corrugated holes at one end of the cardboard. You can use fancier clips if you have them.

3. Fasten your worksheet or drawing paper under the clips, and voila! You have a working clipboard.

HOW TO MAKE A DAYPACK
Daypacks are highly useful bags you carry on your back, leaving your arms free to swing naturally as you walk, and your hands empty and ready to

use. A daypack is simple to make. You need only *a piece of fabric 24 × 36 in, a needle and thread, several straight pins, one safety pin,* and *a pair of scissors.* A sewing machine can speed up the project but is not necessary.

1. Measure the fabric as indicated in this diagram.

2. Cut along solid lines and fold along dotted lines. You should end up with three pattern pieces.

3. Placing the right sides of the fabric together, stitch along the rough edges, leaving a 5/8-in seam allowance. Make extra stitches at the corners for reinforcement.

4. Turn the pieces right-side out so the rough seams are hidden inside. To turn the straps right-side out, fasten a safety pin to one end of each tube and push the pin through the inside to the other end.

5. Pin the straps onto the pack, and adjust them to fit the wearer's body size. The pack should rest comfortably across the back of his or her shoulders. Allow some slack. This will be taken up when the pack is filled.

6. Sew straps firmly in place.

Daypack fillers: lunch, extra sweater, bandanna, clipboard or notebook, pens and pencils, crayons or colored markers, plastic bag, small jar for catching and observing insects, one-meter length of string for measuring, hand lens, nature guides, old spoon for digging, gloves for collecting trash.

RESOURCES

BIBLIOGRAPHY

Allen, Patricia R. *Youthbook: Models and Resources for Neighborhood Use.* New York: Citizens Committee for New York City (3 West Twenty-ninth St., New York, NY 10001), 1980. A well-written and beautifully designed resources guide containing over 245 models of programs run for and by young people in New York City. Provides useful, inspiring models for people in any city who wish to develop neighborhood programs for children and young people.

Allison, Linda. *The Reasons for Seasons: The Great Cosmic Megagalactic Trip Without Moving from Your Chair.* Boston: Little, Brown, 1975.

————. *The Wild Inside: Sierra Club's Guide to the Great Indoors.* San Francisco: Sierra Club Books, 1979.

Bekey, Michelle. "Waste: Cleaning Up One of Our Most Serious Issues." *California Business,* July 1982, 53–56, 86–90.

Bense, Beverly, Holly Mines, Jo Mueller, Susan Nemir, and Toby Pohl. *First Steps in Ecology: A Guide for the Elementary Grades.* Berkeley: Ecology Center (1403 Addison St., Berkeley, CA 94702), 1975.

BioCycle: Journal of Waste Recycling. J. G. Press, Emmaus, PA 18049. Best source for information on local and regional composting of discards ranging from sewage sludge to plant materials.

Brandwein, Judith. *Dress Up Your Neighborhood.* New York: Citizens Committee for New York City (3 West Twenty-ninth St., New York, NY 10001), 1979.

Children and Animals: Better Teaching Through Humane Education. Box 362, East Haddam, CT 06423. A magazine published four times during the school year by the National Association for the Advancement of Humane Education, a division of the Humane Society of the United States. Written for adults, it includes stories and other learning activities for children.

Children's Environments Quarterly (formerly *Childhood City Newsletter*). Center for Human Environments, Graduate Center CUNY, 33 West Forty-second St., New York, NY 10036.

Cornell, Joseph Bharat. *Sharing Nature with Children: A Parents' and Teachers' Nature-Awareness Guidebook.* Nevada City, Calif.: Ananda Publications, 1979. An attractive, well-designed guide chock full of imaginative games yet small enough to fit in a back pocket. Each activity is coded so users can see at a glance which ones will work for their group.

Editors of *Reader's Digest. The Living World of Nature.* New York: Berkley Books, 1980.

Environmental Action Coalition. *City Trees, Country Trees.* New York: Environmental Action Coalition (625 Broadway, New York, NY 10012), n.d. See Organizations for a list of other booklets on the urban environment available through the coalition.

Farb, Peter. *The Living Earth.* New York: Harper & Row, 1959.

Farrallones Institute. *The Integral Urban House: Self-Reliant Living in the City.* San Francisco: Sierra Club Books, 1979.

Fiarotta, Phyllis. *Snips and Snails and Walnut Whales: Nature Crafts for Children.* New York: Workman, 1975.

Gorrell, Nancy. *The Lone Recycler.* Berkeley: Materials World Publishing (1329 Hopkins St., Berkeley, CA 94702), 1984. A comic book on recycling for kids nine years old and up.

Group for Environmental Education. *Our Man-Made Environment, Book Seven.* Cambridge: MIT Press, 1970. One of the few books we found designed to introduce children to the built environment. Presents concepts through problem-solving exercises and encourages explorations of physical environments. Part of a series that introduces children to the process of choice involved in shaping their built environments.

Hyde, Margaret O. *Animal Clocks and Compasses.* New York: McGraw-Hill, 1960.

Jeavons, John. *How To Grow More Vegetables Than You Ever Thought Possible on Less Land Than You Can Imagine.* Berkeley: Ten Speed Press, 1979. A primer on the biodynamic/French intensive method of organic horticulture.

Jones, W. Ron. *Your City Has Been Kidnapped.* Deschool Primer No. 3. San Francisco: Zephyros, 1972. This and other publications in the series served as a major inspiration for our city explorations. Unfortunately, the primers are no longer in print.

Katz, Adrienne. *Naturewatch: Exploring Nature with Your Children.* Reading, Mass.: Addison-Wesley, 1986.

KIND News. Box 362, East Haddam, CT 06423. A periodical for kids in grades 2 through 6, published by the National Association for the Advancement of Humane Education, a division of the Humane Society of the United States.

Kirshner, Dan, and Adam Stern. *To Burn or Not to Burn: The Economic Advantages of Recycling over Garbage Incineration for New York City.* New York: The Environmental Defense Fund (444 Park Ave. S., New York, NY 10016), 1985.

Knapp, Daniel, and Mary Lou Van Deventer. *A Handbook of Recycling* (working title). Berkeley and Los Angeles: University of California Press, forthcoming.

Lawrence Hall of Science. *Outdoor Biology Instructional Strategies (OBIS).* Nashua, N.H.: Delta Education (Box

M, Nashua, NH 03061), 1981. OBIS is an excellent
outdoor program that offers young people fun and
challenging opportunities to investigate ecological
relationships in their local environment. The
ninety-seven OBIS activities, which take youngsters
outdoors to investigate biology and to increase their
environmental awareness, are available in modules or
individually. Although designed for youngsters ten to
fifteen years of age, the strategies have been used
successfully by younger and older participants,
including families. You can conduct the activities at
almost any time of day and in any season and weather.

Macaulay, David. *City: A Story of Roman Planning and
Construction.* Boston: Houghton Mifflin, 1976. This and
the following award-winning children's books by
Macauley, all coffee table size, include extensive and
detailed illustrations of the built environment.

————. *Unbuilding.* Ibid., 1980. Shows how skyscrapers
and highrises are demolished.

————. *Underground.* Ibid., 1974. A fascinating illustrated
exploration of the complex and immense system of
walls, columns, cables, pipes, and tunnels that exists
beneath the buildings and streets of a modern city.

Moskowitz, Milton, Michael Katz, and Robert Levering,
eds. *Everybody's Business: An Almanac—The Irreverent
Guide to Corporate America.* San Francisco: Harper &
Row, 1980. Filled with entertaining and well-researched
facts about the rise of major corporations in the United
States. Includes statistics on the consumption of
products and the growth of industries.

National Association for the Advancement of Humane
Education. *People and Animals.* East Haddam, Conn.:
National Association for the Advancement of Humane
Education (Box 362, East Haddam, CT 06423), 1981. A
binder-format curriculum guide for use with grades 2
through 6.

National Center for Appropriate Technology.
Connections: A Curriculum in Appropriate Technology

for the Fifth and Sixth Grades. Butte, Mont.: National Center for Appropriate Technology (P.O. Box 3838, Butte MT 59702), 1980.

Rights, Molly. *Beastly Neighbors: All About Wild Things in the City, or Why Earwigs Make Good Mothers.* Boston: Little, Brown, 1981.

Rublowsky, John. *Nature in the City.* New York: Basic Books, 1967.

Schlitz Audubon Center. *Living Lightly in the City.* Milwaukee: Schlitz Audubon Center (1111 East Brown Deer Rd., Milwaukee, WI 53217), 1983. A curriculum guide for grades K through 6.

———. *Living Lightly on the Planet.* Ibid. 1985. A two-volume curriculum guide for grades 7 through 12.

Simon, Seymour. *Pets in a Jar: Collecting and Caring for Small Wild Animals.* New York: Penguin Books, 1975.

Simons, Robin. *Recyclopedia: Games, Science Equipment, and Crafts from Recycled Materials.* Boston: Houghton Mifflin, 1976.

Smith, Judy. *Something Old, Something New, Something Borrowed, Something Due: Women in Appropriate Technology.* Butte, Mont.: Center For Appropriate Technology (P.O. Box 3838, Butte, MT 59702), 1978.

Storer, John H. *The Web of Life.* New York: Devin Adair, 1954.

Urban Bikeway Design Collaborative. *Cyclateral Thinking: An Atlas of Ideas for Bicycle Planning.* Cambridge, 1976. No longer in print.

Wahrhaftig, Clyde. *Streetcar to Subduction.* Washington, D.C.: American Geophysical Union, 1984. A walker's guide to the geology of San Francisco. Includes not only the rock underfoot but also the stone used in building facades. The predecessor to this book was a special issue of *Mineral Information Service* written by the author and a colleague in 1966. (See following entry.)

Wahrhaftig, Clyde, and Gordon Oakeshott. "The Walker's Guide to the Geology of San Francisco." *Mineral*

Information Service (now *California Geology*), November 1966. Still available through the California Division of Mines and Geology, 380 Civic Dr., Suite 100, Pleasant Hill, CA 94523.

Washington State Office of Public Instruction. *Encounters with The Northwest Environment.* Seattle, 1981. (Available through the Washington State Office of Environmental Education, N.W. Section, 17011 Meridian Ave. N., Seattle, WA 98133.) This curriculum guide provides a framework for exploring both rural and urban environments in the Pacific Northwest. It uses Seattle as a model for teaching how a city works. Although designed for high school students, the guide can be modified for younger children. For a catalog of other environmental curriculum guides and learning resources, write the Washington State Office of Environmental Education.

————. *Energy, Food, and You: An Interdisciplinary Curriculum Guide for Secondary Schools.* Seattle, 1981. (Available through the Washington State Office of Environmental Education, N.W. Section, 17011 Meridian Ave. N., Seattle, WA 98133.) Filled with detailed, well-documented activities for studying the relationship between energy and food. Presents and interprets information usually found only in government reports and scholarly journals. An elementary school version is also available.

Welty, Joel Carl. *The Life of Birds.* Philadelphia: W. B. Saunders, 1962.

Westland, Cor, and Jane Knight. *Playing, Living, Learning: A Worldwide Perspective on Children's Opportunities to Play.* Pennsylvania: Venture, 1982. A compilation of hundreds of experiments in children's play being conducted from Denmark to Hong Kong to Argentina. Includes everything from children's farms to New Games to playstreets.

Wigglesworth, V. B. *The Life of Insects.* New York: Mentor Books, 1968.

Williams, Linda Verlee. *Teaching for the Two-Sided Mind.*
Englewood Cliffs, N.J.: Prentice-Hall, 1983. An excellent
summary of current research and discussion of its
implications for education. Includes scores of practical
teaching techniques that draw upon the brain's right
hemisphere, using visual thinking, fantasy, metaphor,
music and more.

FILM

Toast. Daniel Hoffman, Earth Chronicles, copyright 1974,
released 1977. (Available through BullFrog Films, Oley,
PA 19547. Telephone: 215-779-8226.) This twelve-minute
prizewinning film depicts the energy required to
produce and use a store-bought loaf of bread—from
planting and harvesting the grain to driving to the store
to toasting a slice. Lively soundtrack, few words.

ORGANIZATIONS

Ecology Center, 1430 Addison St., Berkeley, CA 94702.
Telephone: 415-548-2220. Ongoing programs include a
switchboard clearing house of environmental
information, a bookstore, curbside recycling pickup, a
newsletter, a library, and publications about gardening,
composting, and raising food animals in an urban area.

Environmental Action Coalition, 625 Broadway, New
York, NY 10012. Telephone: 212-677-1601. Publishes free
curriculum materials, including the booklets *Green
Spaces in City Places; City Trees, Country Trees; Plant a
Tree for Arbor Day;* and *Woods and Water.* Also
distributes *Eco News,* a children's publication.

Girl Scouts of the USA, 830 Third Ave., New York, NY
10022. Telephone: 212-940-7500. Has developed a broad
environmental education program that includes
publications and films on improving the environment
through such activities as building trails, cleaning up
polluted rivers, and developing sites into outdoor
environmental learning areas. The national office offers
grants from the Reader's Digest Foundation to troops
engaged in environmental projects.

Inner City Outings, a program of the *Sierra Club,* 730 Polk St., San Francisco, CA 94109. Telephone: 415-923-5628. Helps coordinate twenty-three volunteer groups in cities throughout the United States. The groups provide wilderness experiences for disadvantaged urban kids, senior citizens, and the disabled.

International Association for the Child's Right to Play. Council Representative: Robin Moore, School of Design, North Carolina State University, P.O. Box 5398, Raleigh, NC 27650. Telephone: 919-737-2204. Provides an international forum and advocacy for the promotion of play opportunities for all children. Specific interests include environments for play, leisure time facilities, programs that develop the whole child, play leadership training, and toys and play materials. A new project focuses on peace and war toys and how they affect play, growth, and the development of the child.

National Association for the Advancement of Humane Education, a division of the Humane Society of the United States, P.O. Box 362, East Haddam, CT 06423. Telephone: 203-434-8666. Publishes curriculum guides for preschool through sixth grade that correlate humane education in math, social studies, science, and language arts. Also publishes *Children and Animals,* a magazine for adults who work with kids, and *KIND News,* a magazine for kids in second through sixth grades.

National Center for Appropriate Technology, 3040 Continental Dr., P.O. Box 3838, Butte, MT 59702. Telephone: 406-494-4572. Answers questions by phone and provides printed material by mail regarding small-scale, environmentally sound, low-cost, locally based approaches to problems that emphasize self-help. Publishes *Connections: A Curriculum in Appropriate Technology for the Fifth and Sixth Grades* and a duplicated reprint of *Something Old, Something New, Something Borrowed, Something Due: Women and Appropriate Technology.*

National Gardening Association, 180 Flynn Ave.,
Burlington, VT 05401. Telephone: 802-863-1308.
Distributes three gardening slide shows: *This Is
Community Gardening; Youth Gardening Slide Show;*
and *Senior Gardening Slide Show.* Publishes the *Youth
Gardening Book* and an excellent monthly gardening
newsmagazine, *National Gardening* (formerly *Gardens
for All*).

National Trust for Historic Preservation, 1785
Massachusetts Ave., N.W., Washington, DC 20026.
Telephone: 202-673-4000. Publishes the newsletter
Conserve Neighborhoods. The September-October 1981
issue, *Neighborhoods Organizing Guide: Ideas for
Bringing Your Neighborhood Together,* is still available.
We recommend it highly.

PLAE, Inc., 1824 Fourth St., Berkeley, CA 94710.
Telephone: 415-845-PLAE. Creates programs and
environments that integrate children of all abilities.
PLAE (Playing and Learning in Adaptable
Environments) develops experiential theme workshops
for schools, parks, recreation centers, and organizations.
In addition, PLAE offers technical assistance in the
design of play and learning environments for all
children; program planning and staff development; and
training for designers, educators, parents, and managers
of recreational environments.

Prospect Park Environment Center, the Picnic House,
Prospect Park, Brooklyn, NY 11215. Telephone:
718-788-8500. Conducts tours of parks and of the built
environment for school groups and for adults.

Shoots 'n Roots, 929 North Sixth Street, Milwaukee, WI
53203. Telephone: 414-224-4866. This group's Urban
Garden Program is designed to help people learn to
grow, serve, and preserve homegrown vegetables. Each
summer it introduces inner-city children to gardening.
Some of these children help disabled elderly people
plant and tend plots. Publishes a newsletter as well as
free fact sheets in both English and Spanish.